THE POWER OF THE SPIRIT

THE

POWER
OF THE SPIRIT

Selections from the Writings of William Law

EDITED BY ANDREW MURRAY

DIMENSION BOOKS
BETHANY FELLOWSHIP, INC.
Minneapolis, Minn. 55438

The Power of the Spirit
by William Law
edited by Andrew Murray

Library of Congress catalog card number: 76-57110

ISBN 0-87123-463-7

Reprinted in 1977 from the James Nisbet & Company
edition of 1896

This edition published in 1977 by Bethany Fellowship, Inc.
6820 Auto Club Road, Minneapolis, Minnesota 55438

Printed in the United States of America

CONTENTS

—◆—

	PAGE
INTRODUCTION	ix

AN ADDRESS TO THE CLERGY.

1. The one thing essential to Salvation: The Power of the Spirit of God in us	1
2. The Holy Spirit thus needed, because all Goodness is in God alone, and inseparable from Him . . .	3
3. True Religion nothing but the continual dependence upon God for all goodness	4
4. The only Good of Religion, the Power and Presence of God working in us	5
5. Nothing can seek God but what comes from Him . .	6
6. All Religion that proceeds not from the Immediate Working of the Divine Nature within us is Selfish and Vain .	8
7. We cannot love God, but with His own Holy Love brought to Life in us	9
8. Divine Inspiration was essential to Man's first created state	10
9. Inspiration must be Immediate and Continual . .	12
10. To believe in Immediate Continual Inspiration is neither Enthusiasm nor Pride	13
11. All Life in Nature bears witness to the Truth of Continual Inspiration	15
12. The Gospel State solely a Ministration of the Spirit .	16
13. No True Knowledge of Redemption but by the Holy Spirit Opening the Mystery of a Redeeming Christ in the Inward Part	18
14. Of the Occasional Influence of the Spirit . .	21
15. Our Salvation only in the Life of Christ Jesus in us .	24

PAGE

16. The Religion of Self or Nature 25
17. Of Grieving and Resisting the Spirit . . . 29
18. All Scripture teaches us our entire dependence upon the Spirit of God 33
19. Of Christ's Coming into our Hearts as a Living, Holy Nature within us 36
20. Both God and Satan have their work within us . . 39
21. The Teaching of the Church on Continual Inspiration . 40
22. Of the Abuse of the Doctrine by Enthusiasts . . 42
23. Of Denying our Reason in Religion as an essential part of Self-denial 43
24. The Use of Reason in Religion 49
25. The Presence of the Holy Spirit means more than the Inspiration of the Holy Scriptures 54
26. The true value of Scripture as an outward Guide to God's inward Teaching 58
27. All Knowledge to be Sacrificed to the Glory of the Gospel . 60
28. Something more than Sound Understanding needed to receive the Teaching of the Spirit . . . 64
29. All Knowledge of the Spirit dependent upon His dwelling in us 67
30. Only the Holy Spirit can give the Real Possession of what Scripture relates 69
31. The Difference between a mere Letter-learned Knowledge and that which the Divine Life within us gives . . 71
32. The Kingdom of God is only where the Light and Spirit of God dwell and rule 76
33. Trust in the Wisdom of Men the cause of the Fall of the Church from its first state 78
34. Of Self. The Denial of our own Wisdom the chief part of Self-denial 80
35. Of Pride and Humility, and the reason why the need of Self-denial is so absolute 85
36. Natural Reason and the Glory of Learning the great Stronghold of Self and Pride 89
37. The true nature of the Kingdom of Heaven . . 93
38. Man needs to be Saved from his own Wisdom as much as from his own Righteousness 95
39. The Letter killeth, but the Spirit giveth Life . . 97
40. The distinction between Literal and Divine Knowledge almost lost in the Christian Church . . . 99
41. Love the only Key to true Knowledge . . . 104

PAGE

42. Human Wisdom, without the Light of God born in the
    Soul, is but the Darkness of Nature . . . 109
43. We need the Fire and Spirit of Heaven . . . 110
44. The Kingdom of God is within you 113
45. The Christian, not owning the Holy Spirit as the fulfil-
    ling of the Gospel, is in the same fallen state as the
    Jew not owning Christ as the fulfilling of the Law . 116
46. Of Mistaking the Outward for the Inward . . . 118
47. The Cause of all Blindness in the Church as in Paradise,
    the desire of other Knowledge than comes from God
    alone 120
48. Only he that loveth, knoweth God 122
49. The Departure from the one Mystic Way of Salvation the
    cause of the Corruption of Christendom . . . 124
50. No true Church Reformation but in departing from the
    Spirit of the World 125
51. Holiness the Sole End of the Church 128
52. The Mark of true Church Membership being dead unto
    all Sin 129
53. Of the Necessity of Sinning 132
54. All Human Imperfection will prevail as much in the
    Church as in any Human Society, until we know a
    Continual Inspiration as the power of Deliverance
    from Sin 135
55. The True Salvation Church 136
56. The New Life by the Holy Spirit living in us, the Sole
    End of Christ's coming 139

ADDITIONAL EXTRACTS.

1. The Spirit of the World and the Spirit of God . . 141
2. No True Religion but by the Spirit of God . . . 144
3. The Gospel, a Ministration of the Spirit . . . 147
4. Reason and Faith 151

LETTER I.

5. Of the Inward and Outward Church . . . 157
6. Of Spiritual Worship 160
7. How to Become Spiritual Worshippers . . . 163
8. Of the Imperfection of Churches 165

CONTENTS

LETTER II.

PAGE

9. The first business of a Clergyman 168
10. The first object of Preaching, to stir up the Inward
    Hearing of the Heart 174
11. The great Work of the Preacher, to lead Men to the Holy
    Spirit 176

LETTER VI.

12. How to be in the Truth 179
13. How to find the Continual Guidance of the Holy Spirit . 182
14. Redemption, the restoration of the lost Knowledge of
    God, as essentially living and working in the Soul . 184

LETTER X.

15. Of a Sense of Sin 188
16. How Christ is to be Found 193

LETTER XI.

17. Man's Two Enemies: Self and the World . . . 197
18. The Infinite Love of God 198
19. Of giving up all for God 204

LETTER XXV.

20. How Good and Evil are both from God . . . 210
21. How the Life of God is revealed in us . . . 214

INTRODUCTION

———◆———

In publishing the new volume of Law's works, I owe a word of explanation to the Christian public, and all the more because some with whom I feel closely united have expressed their doubt of the wisdom of giving greater currency to the writings of an author who differs markedly in some points from what we hold to be fundamental doctrines of the evangelical faith.

First of all, let me say that, as in publishing the former volume, so now in issuing this, I only do so because I do not know where to find anywhere else the same clear and powerful statement of the truth which the Church needs at the present day. I have tried to read or consult every book I knew of that treats of the work of the Holy Spirit, and nowhere have I met with anything that brings the truth of our dependence on the continual leading of the Spirit, and the assurance that that leading can be enjoyed without interruption, so home to the heart as the teaching of the present volume. It is because I believe that teaching to be entirely scriptural, and to supply what many are looking for, that I venture to recommend it. I do so in the confidence that no one will think that I have done so because I consider the truths he denies matters of minor importance, or have any sympathy with his views.

Perhaps it may be well that I state the point of view from which I regard the matter. In all our thoughts of God we look at Him in a twofold light: either as dwelling above us and without us, Creator, Lawgiver, and Judge, or as dwelling and working within us by His Spirit. In redemption the two aspects find their expression in the two great doctrines of justification and regeneration. In the former, God is regarded as a Judge, as separate from us, as much against us in law, and occupying very much the same relation as any judge on earth towards the accused he sentences. In justification, grace forgives and accepts. In regeneration, the work of redemption is regarded from an entirely different point of view. Sin is death, the loss of the divine life; grace is seen as the new life implanted by the Holy Spirit, and by Him maintained in the soul.

It is only in the full and perfect harmony of the two truths, that the glory of grace, or the blessedness of the Christian life, can be fully known. It is seldom given to any human mind to hold two sides of truth with equal clearness; and it has often happened that where one side of truth has laid powerful hold, another aspect has been neglected or denied. This was very markedly the case with WILLIAM LAW. The truth of God's inworking in regeneration, not only as the act of grace by which the divine life is imparted, but in the unceasing maintenance of that life by the working of the indwelling Spirit, so filled his whole soul, that for other truths which did not appear to harmonise with this he had no eye or heart.

But into that portion of truth which he had received he appears to me to have had an insight such as is given to few. I confess that in all my reading I have never found anyone who has so helped me in understanding the Scripture truth of the work of the Holy Spirit. And it is because I know of no one who has put certain aspects of needed truth with the same clearness, that I cannot but think that he is a messenger from God to call His Church to give the blessed Spirit the place of honour that belongs to Him.

As I have studied this Address to the Clergy I have thought I learnt to understand better than ever before what the relation is which the work of the Holy Spirit bears to the Father and the Son, as well as to the Church and the believer. Law begins by taking us back to the Being of God, and showing how His very nature as God implies that He is the only source of life and power; how they are eternally inseparable from Himself, and how therefore all life and power in the universe are nothing but the direct and continuous working of God. It shows how, both in angels and men, the true relation of the creature, all true religion in heaven and earth, consists in nothing but an absolute and unalterable dependence upon God, and how the highest blessedness is nothing but the most complete surrender to let this blessed God do His work. He proves how all the work of Christ had no other object than to restore this blessed relation, and to secure the immediate and unceasing working of the Holy Spirit as the one condition for the full experience of the power of His redemption. And he leads us to see how in the promise of the Holy Spirit given by our Lord, and the personal experience and witness of His indwelling, we have the one secret of the power of Christ's Church, of the ministry of the Word, and of the individual believer.

What my own experience has taught me has been confirmed by observation in intercourse with others, that it is very possible to be in earnest in seeking for the Spirit's working, while there is very little apprehension of the absoluteness of His claim. If we understood how it is His alone to communicate to us what we are to know and enjoy of God and Christ; how it is by Him alone that we can ever live in the will or the love of God; how it is by Him most surely that, just as our life is maintained by the air we breathe each moment, our spiritual life can indeed be in the power of the endless life of heaven; our dependence on Him, our prayer for His operation, our trust in

Him, and our life would be so different from what it is. All this will, I think, come much more, as we see the deep divine reasonableness and beauty of the place given in the holy Trinity to the Spirit as the Third, the Great Consummator and Communicator of what the Father planned and the Son worked out.

In some respects no two men differ more than John Calvin and William Law. The latter repudiates the teaching of the former. And yet no one reminds me more of Calvin than Law. Calvin's theology had but one thought, the glory of God, and our absolute dependence upon Him. The shape this principle took in his teaching of the Predestinating Sovereignty of Grace, Law entirely rejects. And yet, I have nowhere met a teacher who, from another side, has opened up this same truth of the Glory of God and our absolute dependence on Him, as Law. The glory of God, as being throughout the universe and throughout eternity, the only source of goodness and of power, is so magnified by him that the thought of absolute dependence is seen to be the very necessity and the very blessedness of our being. Often the thought has come to me of seeing Calvin and Law in heaven very near each other, side by side, in deepest prostration, special witnesses to that absolute dependence which alone can bring God the glory due to His name.

During my stay in England I have been surprised at the response that a very simple message on *Waiting on God* has met with. I find multitudes who long to know more of it. Its secret and joy will be found in knowing God Himself better. I cannot say how much I owe to this volume of Law in showing me, from the very nature of God, how waiting on Him is the very beginning, as it is the highest attainment in true religion.

The connection between this and the work of the Holy Spirit will be easily seen. He is the mighty power of God. He is now the power of the redeeming God in Christ working in us. In Him God will reveal Himself in us, will with His Son dwell in us, and fill our hearts with His love. I am confident we have no conception of the change that would come if, with one heart and one soul, we were to take our place with the first disciples at the footstool of our ascended Lord, and with one accord claim the promised gift.

The book is an Address to the Clergy. Its opening paragraph, " The power of the Spirit of God in us, the one thing essential to salvation," is an appeal to ministers to see that they do not miss that which is the most essential part of their message and work. I ask the help of all who learn to value the book to bring it to the notice of those who preach the gospel. I beg of my brethren in the ministry to give it no cursory perusal. The line of thought may perhaps be foreign to what modern religious literature has taught them. I am confident a patient and prayerful perusal will bring a rich blessing. If any would wish to have the sum of the whole ere they begin, they will

find it in the additional extracts in this volume, pars.
9–11 (pp. 168–178). I can hardly think that
anything could be found more intensely interesting
and instructive than this letter to a clergyman.

But the book is for all Christians. The want of
our religion is that there is too little personal dealing
with God. Our faith stands more in the wisdom of
men than in the power of God. There is no need so
crying as that believers be taught how to meet with
God, to tarry and to dwell with Him. This the Holy
Spirit alone can do. But this book can be as a voice
in the wilderness. Prepare ye the way of the Lord;
make straight A HIGHWAY FOR OUR GOD. It has brought
so much light and blessing to myself, that I cannot
but urge all who long for a deeper life to listen to its
instructions.

The one need of our churches, of our life, and our
work, is, *the continuous operation of the Holy Spirit.*
That one promise of the Father through His blessed
Son is *the continuous operation of the Holy Spirit.*
Shall we not say that the one cry of our heart and the
one study of our life shall be, how to live in such simple,
absolute dependence upon God, that the continuous
operation of the Holy Spirit may be our blessed portion.

That God may visit His Church, and fill all His
saints with His Holy Spirit, is my fervent prayer.

                                        ANDREW MURRAY.

WIMBLEDON, 4th December 1895.

WILLIAM LAW was an English clergyman who lived in the era just preceding the American Revolution. He lost his job at Cambridge for refusing to take an oath of allegiance to King George. The subsequent black-listing by the state church gave him ample time for prayer, contemplation and writing.

THE POWER OF THE HOLY SPIRIT.

AN ADDRESS TO THE CLERGY.

1. The one thing essential to Salvation: The Power of the Spirit of God in us.

THE reason of my humbly and affectionately addressing this Discourse to the Clergy, is not because it treats of things not of common concern to all Christians, but chiefly to invite and induce them, as far as I can, to the serious perusal of it; and because whatever is essential to Christian salvation, if either neglected, overlooked, or mistaken by them, is of the saddest consequence both to themselves and the churches in which they minister. I say essential to salvation, for I would not turn my own thoughts, or call the attention of Christians, to anything but the one thing needful, the one thing essential and only available to our rising out of our fallen state, and becoming, as we were at our creation, an holy offspring of God, and real partakers of the divine nature.

If it be asked, What this one thing is? It is the SPIRIT OF GOD brought again to HIS FIRST POWER OF LIFE IN US. Nothing else is wanted

by us, nothing else is intended for us, by the Law,
the Prophets, and the Gospel. Nothing else is, or
can be effectual, to the making sinful man become
again a godly creature.

Everything else, be it what it will, however
glorious and divine in outward appearance, everything that angels, men, churches, or reformations,
can do for us, is dead and helpless, but so far as it
is the immediate work of the Spirit of God breathing
and living in it.

All Scripture bears full witness to this truth, and
the end and design of all that is written, is only to
call us back from the spirit of Satan, the flesh, and
the world, to be again under full dependence upon,
and obedience to the Spirit of God, who out of free
love and thirst after our souls, seeks to have His first
power of life in us. When this is done, all is done
that the Scripture can do for us. Read what chapter,
or doctrine of Scripture you will, be ever so delighted
with it, it will leave you as poor, as empty, and
unreformed as it found you, unless it be a delight
that proceeds from, and has turned you wholly and
solely to the Spirit of God, and strengthened your
union with and dependence upon Him. For love and
delight in matters of Scripture, whilst it is only a
delight that is merely human, however specious and
saintlike it may appear, is but the self-love of fallen
Adam, and can have no better a nature, till it
proceeds from the inspiration of God, quickening His
own life and nature within us, which alone can have
or give forth a godly love. For if it be an immutable
truth, that " no man can call Jesus, Lord, but by the
Holy Ghost," it must be a truth equally immutable,

that no one can have any one Christlike temper or power of goodness, but so far, and in such degree, as he is immediately led and governed by the Holy Spirit.

2. The Holy Spirit thus needed, because all Goodness is in God alone, and inseparable from Him.

The grounds and reasons of which are as follow :—

All possible goodness that either can be named, or is nameless, was in God from all eternity, and must to all eternity be inseparable from Him; it can be nowhere but where God is. As therefore before God created anything, it was certainly true that there was but one that was good, so it is just the same truth, after God has created innumerable hosts of blessed holy and heavenly beings, that there is but one that is good, and that is God.

All that can be called goodness, holiness, divine tempers, heavenly affections, etc., in the creatures, are no more their own, or the growth of their created powers, than they were their own before they were created. But all that is called divine goodness and virtue in the creature is nothing else, but the one goodness of God manifesting a birth and discovery of itself in the creature, according as its created nature is fitted to receive it. This is the unalterable state between God and the creature. Goodness for ever and ever can only belong to God, as essential to Him and inseparable from Him, as His own unity.

God could not make the creature to be great and glorious in itself; this is as impossible, as for God to create beings into a state of independence on

Himself. "The Heavens," saith David, "declare the glory of God"; and no creature, any more than the Heavens, can declare any other glory but that of God. And as well might it be said, that the firmament shows forth its own handy-work, as that a holy divine or heavenly creature shows forth its own natural power.

3. True Religion nothing but the continual dependence upon God for all goodness.

But now, if all that is divine, great, glorious, and happy, in the spirits, tempers, operations, and enjoyments of the creature, is only so much of the greatness, glory, majesty, and blessedness of God, dwelling in it, and giving forth various births of his own triune life, light, and love, in and through the manifold forms and capacities of the creature to receive them, then we may infallibly see the true ground and nature of all true religion, and when and how we may be said to fulfil all our religious duty to God. For the creature's true religion is its rendering to God all that is God's, it is its true continual acknowledging all that which it is, and has, and enjoys, in and from God. This is the one true religion of all intelligent creatures, whether in heaven, or on earth; for as they all have but one and the same relation to God, so though ever so different in their several births, states, or offices, they all have but one and the same true religion, or right behaviour towards God. Now, the one relation, which is the ground of all true religion, and is one and the same between God and all intelligent creatures, is this, it is a total unalterable dependence upon God, an immediate continual receiving of every

kind and degree of goodness, blessing, and happiness
that ever was, or can be found in them, from God
alone. The highest angel has nothing of its own that
it can offer unto God, no more light, love, purity,
perfection, and glorious hallelujahs, that spring from
itself, or its own powers, than the poorest creature
upon earth. Could the angel see a spark of wisdom,
goodness, or excellence, as coming from, or belonging
to itself, its place in heaven would be lost, as sure as
Lucifer lost his. But they are ever-abiding flames of
pure love, always ascending up to and uniting with
God, for this reason, because the wisdom, the power,
the glory, the majesty, the love, and goodness of God
alone, is all that they see, and feel, and know, either
within or without themselves. Songs of praise to
their heavenly Father are their ravishing delight,
because they see, and know, and feel that it is the
breath and spirit of their heavenly Father that sings
and rejoices in them. Their adoration in spirit and
in truth never ceases, because they never cease to
acknowledge the all of God; the all of God in themselves, and the all of God in the whole creation. This
is the one religion of heaven, and nothing else is the
truth of religion on earth.

4. The only Good of Religion, the Power and Presence of God working in us.

The matter therefore plainly comes to this, nothing
can do, or be, the good of religion to the intelligent
creature, but the power and presence of God really
and essentially living and working in it. But if this
be the unchangeable nature of that goodness and

blessedness which is to be had from our religion, then of all necessity, the creature must have all its religious goodness as wholly and solely from God's immediate operation, as it had its first goodness at its creation. And it is the same impossibility for the creature to help itself to that which is good and blessed in religion, by any contrivance, reasonings, or workings of its own natural powers, as to create itself. For the creature, after its creation, can no more take anything to itself that belongs to God, than it could take it before it was created. And if truth forces us to hold that the natural powers of the creature could only come from the one power of God, the same truth should surely more force us to confess, that that which comforts, that which enlightens, that which blesses, which gives peace, joy, goodness, and rest to its natural powers, can be had in no other way, nor by any other thing, but from God's immediate holy operation found in it.

5. Nothing can seek God but what comes from Him.

Now the reason why no work of religion, but that which is begun, continued, and carried on by the living operation of God in the creature, can have any truth, goodness, or divine blessing in it, is because nothing can in truth seek God, but that which comes from God. Nothing can in truth find God as its good, but that which has the nature of God living in it, like can only rejoice in like; and therefore no religious service of the creature can have any truth, goodness, or blessing in it, but that which is done in the creature, in, and through, and by a principle and power of the divine nature begotten and breathing forth in it all holy tempers, affections, and adorations.

All true religion is, or brings forth, an essential union and communion of the spirit of the creature with the spirit of the Creator: God in it, and it in God, one life, one light, one love. The Spirit of God first gives, or sows the seed of divine union in the soul of every man; and religion is that by which it is quickened, raised, and brought forth to a fulness and growth of a life in God. Take a similitude of this, as follows. The beginning, or seed of animal breath, must first be born in the creature from the spirit of this world, and then respiration, so long as it lasts, keeps up an essential union of the animal life with the breath or spirit of this world. In like manner, divine faith, hope, love, and resignation to God, are in the religious life its acts of respiration, which, so long as they are true, unite God and the creature in the same living and essential manner, as animal respiration unites the breath of the animal with the breath of this world.

Now, as no animal could begin to respire, or unite with the breath of this world, but because it has its beginning to breathe begotten in it from the air of this world, so it is equally certain that no creature, angel, or man could begin to be religious, or breathe forth the divine affections of faith, love, and desire towards God, but because a living seed of these divine affections was by the Spirit of God first begotten in it. And as a tree or plant can only grow and fructify by the same power that first gave birth to the seed, so faith, and hope, and love towards God, can only grow and fructify by the same power, that begot the first seed of them in the soul. Therefore divine

immediate inspiration and divine religion are inseparable in the nature of the thing.

Take away inspiration, or suppose it to cease, and
then no religious acts or affections can give forth anything that is godly or divine. For the creature can
offer, or return nothing to God, but that which it has
first received from Him; therefore, if it is to offer and
send up to God affections and aspirations that are
divine and godly, it must of all necessity have the
divine and godly nature living and breathing in it.
Can anything reflect light before it has received it?
Or any other light than that which it has received?
Can any creature breathe forth earthly, or diabolical
affection, before it is possessed of an earthly, or diabolical
nature? Yet this is as possible, as for any creature
to have divine affections rising up and dwelling in it,
either before, or any further, than as it has or partakes
of the divine nature dwelling and operating in it.

6. All Religion that proceeds not from the Immediate Working of the Divine Nature within us is Selfish and Vain.

A religious faith that is uninspired, a hope, or love
that proceeds not from the immediate working of the
divine nature within us, can no more do any divine
good to our souls, or unite them with the goodness of
God, than an hunger after earthly food can feed us with
the immortal bread of heaven. All that the natural
or uninspired man does, or can do in the Church,
has no more of the truth or power of divine worship
in it than that which he does in the field or shop
through a desire of riches. And the reason is, because

all the acts of the natural man, whether relating to matters of religion or the world, must be equally selfish, and there is no possibility of their being otherwise. For self-love, self-esteem, self-seeking, and living wholly to self, are as strictly the whole of all that is or possibly can be in the natural man, as in the natural beast; the one can no more be better, or act above this nature, than the other. Neither can any creature be in a better or higher state than this till something supernatural is found in it; and this supernatural something, called in Scripture the Word, or Spirit, or Inspiration of God, is that alone from which man can have the first good thought about God, or the least power of having more heavenly desires in his spirit than he has in his flesh.

A religion that is not wholly built upon this supernatural ground, but solely stands upon the powers, reasonings, and conclusions of the natural uninspired man, has not so much as the shadow of true religion in it, but is a mere nothing, in the same sense, as an idol is said to be nothing, because the idol has nothing of that in it which is pretended by it. For the work of religion has no divine good in it, but as it brings forth, and keeps up essential union of the spirit of man with the Spirit of God; which essential union cannot be made, but through love on both sides, nor by love, but where the love that works on both sides is of the same nature.

7. We cannot love God, but with His own Holy Love brought to Life in us.

No man, therefore, can reach God with his love, or have union with Him by it, but he who is inspired

with that one same spirit of love, with which God
loved Himself from all eternity, and before there was
any creature.　Infinite hosts of new created heavenly
beings can begin no new kind of love of God, nor
have the least power of beginning to love Him at all,
but so far as His own Holy Spirit of love, wherewith
He hath from all eternity loved Himself, is brought
to life in them.　This love, that was then in God
alone, can be the only love in creatures that can draw
them to God; they can have no power of cleaving to
Him, of willing that which He wills, or adoring the
divine nature, but by **partaking of that eternal spirit
of love**; and therefore the continual immediate inspiration or operation of the Holy Spirit, is the one
only possible ground of our continually loving God.
And of this inspired love, and no other, it is that
St. John says, " He that dwelleth in love, dwelleth
in God."　Suppose it to be any other love, brought
forth by any other thing but the Spirit of God
breathing His own love in us, and then it cannot
be true that he who dwells in such love, dwells
in God.

8. Divine Inspiration was essential to Man's first created state.

Divine inspiration was essential to man's first
created state.　The Spirit of the triune God, breathed
into, or brought to life in him, was that alone which
made him a holy creature in the image and likeness
of God.　To have no other mover, to live under no
other guide or leader, but the Spirit, was that which
constituted all the holiness which the first man could

have from God. Had he not been thus at the first, God in him and he in God, brought into the world as a true offspring and real birth of the Holy Spirit, no dispensation of glory to fallen man would have directed him to the Holy Spirit, or ever have made mention of His inspiration in man. For fallen man could be directed to nothing as his good, but that which he had, and was his good, before he fell. And had not the Holy Spirit been his first life, in and by which he lived, no inspired prophets among the sons of fallen Adam had ever been heard of, or any holy men speaking as they were moved by the Holy Ghost. For the thing would have been impossible; no fallen man could have been inspired by the Holy Spirit, but because the first life of man was a true and real birth of it; and also because every fallen man had, by the mercy and free grace of God, a secret remains of his first life preserved in him, though hidden, or rather swallowed up by flesh and blood; which secret remains, signified and assured to Adam by the name of a bruiser of the serpent, or seed of the woman, was his only capacity to be called and quickened again into his first life, by new breathings of the Holy Spirit in him.

Hence it plainly appears, that the gospel state could not be God's last dispensation, or the finishing of man's redemption, unless its whole work was a work of the Spirit of God in the spirit of man,— that is, unless without all veils, types, and shadows, it brought the thing itself, or the substance of all former types and shadows, into real enjoyment, so as to be possessed by man in spirit, and in truth. Now the thing itself, and for the sake of which all God's

dispensations have been, is that first life of God
which was essentially born in the soul of the first
man, Adam, and to which he died.

9. Inspiration must be Immediate and Continual.

But now, if the gospel dispensation comes at the
end of all types and shadows, to bring forth again in
man a true and full birth of that Holy Spirit which
he had at first, then it must be plain, that the work
of this dispensation must be solely and immediately
the work of the Holy Spirit.   For if man could no
other possible way have had a holy nature and spirit
at first, but as an offspring or birth of the Holy Spirit
at his creation, it is certain from the nature of the
thing, that fallen man, dead to his first holy nature,
can have that same holy nature again no other way,
but solely by the operation of that same Holy Spirit,
from the breath of which he had at first a holy nature
and life in God.   Therefore, immediate inspiration is as
necessary to make fallen man alive again unto God, as
it was to make man at first a living soul after the image
and in the likeness of God.   And continual inspiration
is as necessary, as man's continuance in his redeemed
state.   For this is a certain truth, that that alone
which begins or gives life, must of all necessity be
the only continuance or preservation of life.   The
second step can only be taken by that which gave
power to take the first.   No life can continue in the
goodness of its first created or redeemed state, but by
its continuing under the influence of, and working with
and by that powerful root or spirit which at first created

or redeemed it. Every branch of the tree, though ever so richly brought forth, must wither and die, as soon as it ceases to have continual union with, and virtue from that root, which first brought it forth. And to this truth, as absolutely grounded in the nature of the thing, our Lord appeals as a proof and full illustration of the necessity of His immediate indwelling, breathing, and operating in the redeemed soul of man, saying, "I am the vine, ye are the branches ; as the branch cannot bear fruit of itself, no more can ye, except ye abide in Me. He that abideth in Me, and I in him, the same bringeth forth much fruit. If a man abides not in Me, he is cast forth as a withered branch ; for without Me, ye can do nothing" (John xv.).

10. To believe in Immediate Continual Inspiration is neither Enthusiasm nor Pride.

Now from these words let this conclusion be here drawn, namely, that, therefore, to turn to Christ as a light within us, to expect life from nothing but His holy birth raised within us, to give ourselves up wholly and solely to the immediate continual influx and operation of His Holy Spirit, depending wholly upon it for every kind and degree of goodness and holiness that we want, or can receive, is, and can be nothing else, but proud, rank enthusiasm.

Now, as infinitely absurd as this conclusion is, no one that condemns continual immediate inspiration as gross enthusiasm, can possibly do it with less absurdity, or show himself a wiser man or better reasoner than he that concludes, that because without Christ we can do nothing, therefore, we ought not to believe, expect, wait for, and depend upon His continual immediate operation in everything that we do, or would do well. As to the pride charged upon this pretended enthusiasm, it is the same absurdity. Christ says, "Without Me ye can do nothing," the same as if He had said, "As to yourselves, and all that can be called your own, you are mere helpless sin and misery, and nothing that is good can come from you, but as it is done by the continual immediate breathing and inspiration of another spirit, given by God to overrule your own, to save and deliver you from all your own goodness, your own wisdom and learning, which always were, and always will be, as corrupt and impure, as earthly and sensual, as your own flesh and blood." Now, is there any selfish, creaturely pride, in fully believing this to be true, and in acting in full conformity to it? If so, then he that confesses he neither has nor ever can have a single farthing, but as it is freely given him from charity, thereby declares himself to be a purse-proud, vain boaster of his own wealth. Such is the spiritual pride of him, who fully acknowledges that he neither has nor can have the least spark or breathing after goodness, but what is freely kindled or breathed into him by the Spirit of God. Again, if it is spiritual pride to believe that nothing that we ever think, or say, or do, either in the Church, or our closets, can have any truth of goodness in it, but that which is wrought solely and immediately by the Spirit of God in us, then it must be said, that in order to have religious humility we must never forget to take some share of our religious virtues to ourselves, and not allow (as Christ hath said) that without Him we can do nothing that is good. It must also be said, that St Paul took too much upon him when he said, " The life that I now live, is not mine, but Christ that liveth in me."

Behold a pride and a humility, the one as good as the other, and both logically descended from a wisdom that confesses it comes not from above.

11. All Life in Nature bears witness to the Truth of Continual Inspiration.

The necessity of a continual inspiration of the Spirit of God, both to begin the first, and continue every step of a divine life in man, is a truth to which every life in nature, as well as all Scripture, bears full witness. A natural life, a bestial life, a diabolical life, can subsist no longer, than whilst they are immediately and continually under the working power of that root or source from which they sprung. Thus it is with the divine life in man, it can never be in him, but as a growth of life in and from God. Hence it is, that resisting the Spirit, quenching the Spirit, grieving the Spirit, is that alone which gives birth and growth to every evil that reigns in the world, and leaves men and churches not only an easy, but a necessary prey to the devil, the world, and the flesh. And nothing but obedience to the Spirit, trusting to the Spirit, walking in the Spirit, praying with and for its continual inspiration, can possibly keep either men or churches from being sinners or idolaters in all that they do. For everything in the life or religion of man that has not the Spirit of God for its mover, director, and

end, be it what it will, is but earthly, sensual, or
devilish.

12. The Gospel State solely a Ministration of the Spirit.

The truth and perfection of the gospel state could
not show itself, till it became solely a ministration of
the spirit, or a kingdom in which the Holy Spirit of
God had the doing of all that was done in it.[1] The
apostles, whilst Christ was with them in the flesh,
were instructed in heavenly truths from His mouth,
and enabled to work miracles in His name, yet not
qualified to know and teach the mysteries of His
kingdom.   After His resurrection, He conversed with
them forty days, speaking to them of things pertain-
ing to the kingdom of God; nay, though He breathed
on them, and said, "Receive ye the Holy Ghost,"
yet this also would not do, they were still unable to
preach, or bear witness to the truth, as it is in Jesus.
And the reason is, there was still a higher dispensation to come, which stood in **such an opening of the
divine life in their hearts,** as could not be effected
from an outward instruction of Christ Himself.   For
though He had sufficiently told His disciples the
necessity of being born again of the Spirit, yet He
left them unborn of it till He came again in the
power of the Spirit.   He breathed on them and said,
"Receive ye the Holy Ghost," yet that which was
said and done, was not the thing itself, but only a
type or outward signification of what they should
receive, when He, being glorified, should come again

[1] Compare the remarkable passage in the Additional Extracts, No. 3.

in the fulness and power of the Spirit, breaking open the deadness and darkness of their hearts with light and life from heaven, which light did, and alone could, open and verify in their souls all that He had said and promised to them whilst He was with them in the flesh. All this is expressly declared by Christ Himself, saying unto them, "I tell you the truth, it is expedient for you that I go away"; therefore Christ taught them to believe the want, and joyfully to expect the coming, of a higher and more blessed state than that of His bodily presence with them. For He adds, "If I go not away, the Comforter will not come"; therefore the comfort and blessing of Christ to His followers could not be had till something more was done to them, and they were brought into a higher state than they could be by His verbal instruction of them. "But if I go away," says He, "I will send Him unto you, and when the Comforter, the Spirit of Truth is come, He will guide you into all truth; He shall glorify Me" (that is, shall set up My kingdom in its glory, in the power of the Spirit), "for He shall receive of Mine, and shall show it unto you: I said of Mine, because all things that the Father hath are Mine" (John xvi.).

Now, when Christ had told them of the necessity of an higher state than that they were in, and the necessity of such a comforting illuminating guide, as they could not have till His outward teaching in human language was changed into the inspiration, and operation of His Spirit in their souls, He commands them not to begin to bear witness of Him to the world from what they did and could in an human way know of Him, His birth, His life, doctrines,

death, sufferings, resurrection, etc., but to tarry at
Jerusalem till they were endued with power from on
high; saying unto them, "Ye shall receive power,
after that the Holy Ghost is come upon you. And
then shall ye bear witness unto Me, both in Jerusalem
and in all Judea, and unto the utmost part of the
earth."

Here are two most important and fundamental
truths fully demonstrated, *First*, that the truth and
perfection of the gospel state could not take place
till Christ was glorified and **His kingdom among men
made wholly and solely a continual immediate ministration of the Spirit**: everything before this was but
subservient for a time, and preparatory to this last
dispensation, which could not have been the last, had
it not carried man above types, figures, and shadows
into the real possession and enjoyment of that which
is the spirit and truth of a divine life. For the end
is not come till it has found the beginning; that is,
the last dispensation of God to fallen man cannot be
come till putting an end to the "bondage of weak
and beggarly elements" (Gal. iv. 9), it brings man to
that dwelling in God, and God in him, which he had
at the beginning.

13. No True Knowledge of Redemption but by the Holy Spirit opening the Mystery of a Redeeming Christ in the Inward Part.

Secondly, That as the apostles could not, so no man,
from their time to the end of the world, can have any
true and real knowledge of the spiritual blessings of

Christ's redemption, or have a divine call, capacity, or fitness to preach and bear witness of them to the world, but solely by that same divine Spirit opening all the mysteries of a redeeming Christ in their inward parts, as it did in the apostles, evangelists, and first ministers of the gospel.

For why could not the apostles, who had been eye-witnesses to all the whole process of Christ, why could they not with their human apprehension declare and testify the truth of such things till they "were baptized with fire and born again of the "Spirit"? It is because the truth of such things, or the mysteries of Christ's process, as knowable by man, are nothing else in themselves but those very things which are done by this heavenly fire and Spirit of God in our souls. Therefore to know the mysteries of Christ's redemption, and to know the redeeming work of God in our own souls, is the same thing; the one cannot be before, or without the other. Therefore every man, be he who he will, however able in all kinds of human literature, must be an entire stranger to all the mysteries of gospel redemption, and can only talk about them as of any other tale he has been told till they are brought forth, verified, fulfilled, and witnessed to by that, which is found, felt, and enjoyed of the whole process of Christ in his soul. For as redemption is in its whole nature an inward spiritual work, that works only in the altering, changing, and regenerating the life of the soul, so it must be true, that nothing but the inward state of the soul can bear true witness to the redeeming power of Christ. For as it wholly consists in altering that which is the most radical in the soul, bringing forth a new spiritual death, and a

new spiritual life, it must be true, that no one can
know or believe the mysteries of Christ's redeeming
power, by historically knowing, or rationally consent-
ing to that which is said of Him and them in written
or spoken words, but only and solely by an inward
experimental finding, and feeling the operation of them,
in that new death, and new life, both of which must
be effected in the soul of man, or Christ is not, cannot
be found and known by the soul as its salvation.   It
must also be equally true, that the redeemed state of
the soul, being in itself nothing else but the resurrection of a divine and holy life in it, must as necessarily from first to last be the sole work of the
breathing, creating Spirit of God, as the first holy
created state of the soul was.   And all this, because
the mysteries of Christ's redeeming power, which work
and bring forth the renewed state of the soul, are not
creaturely, finite, outward things that may be found
and enjoyed by verbal descriptions, or formed ideas of
them, but are a birth and life, and spiritual operation,
which as solely belongs to God alone as His creating
power.   For nothing can redeem, but that same power
which created the soul.   Nothing can bring forth a
good thought in it, but that which brought forth the
power of thinking.   And of every tendency towards
goodness, be it ever so small, that same may be truly
affirmed of it, which St. Paul affirmed of his highest
state, "yet not I, but Christ that liveth in me."

But if the belief of the necessity and certainty of
immediate continual divine inspiration, in and for
everything, that can be holy and good in us, be (as its
accusers say) rank enthusiasm, then he is the only
sober orthodox Christian, who of many a good thought

and action that proceeds from him, frankly says, in order to avoid enthusiasm, my own power, and not Christ's Spirit living and breathing in me, has done this for me. For if all that is good is not done by Christ, then something that is good is done by myself. It is in vain to think that there is a middle way, and that rational divines have found it out, as Dr. Warburton has done, who, though denying immediate continual inspiration, yet allows that the Spirit's "ordinary influence occasionally assists the faithful." [1]

14. Of the Occasional Influence of the Spirit.

Now this middle way has neither Scripture nor sense in it; for an occasional influence or concurrence is as absurd as an occasional God, and necessarily supposes such a God. For an occasional influence of the Spirit upon us supposes an occasional absence of the Spirit from us. For there could be no such thing unless God was sometimes with us and sometimes not, sometimes doing us good, as the inward God of our life, and sometimes doing us no good at all, but leaving us to be good from ourselves. Occasional influence necessarily implies all this blasphemous absurdity. Again, this middle way of an occasional influence and assistance necessarily supposes that there is something of man's own that is good, or the Holy Spirit of God neither would nor could assist or co-operate with it. But if there was anything good in man for God to assist and co-operate with, besides the seed of His own divine nature, or His own word of life striving to

[1] *Sermons*, vol. i.

bruise the serpent's nature within us, it could not be
true that there is only one that is good, and that is
God. And were there any goodness in creatures,
either in heaven, or on earth, but the one goodness of
the divine nature, living, working, and manifesting
itself in them, as its created instruments, then good
creatures, both in heaven and on earth, would have
something else to adore, besides, or along with God.
For goodness, be it where it will, is adorable for itself,
and because it is goodness; if, therefore, any degree of
it belonged to the creature, it ought to have a share of
that same adoration that is paid to the Creator.
Therefore, if to believe that nothing godly can be alive
in us, but what has all its life from the Spirit of God
living and breathing in us, if to look solely to it, and
depend wholly upon it, both for the beginning and
growth of every thought and desire that can be holy
and good in us, be proud, rank enthusiasm, then it
must be the same enthusiasm to own but one God.
For he that owns more goodness than one, owns more
gods than one. And he that believes he can have
any good in him, but the one goodness of God, manifesting itself in him, and through him, owns more
goodness than one. But if it be true, that God and
goodness cannot be divided, then it must be a truth
for ever and ever that so much of good, so much of
God, must be in the creature.

And here lies the true, unchangeable distinction
between God, and nature, and the natural creature.
Nature and creature are only for the outward manifestation of the inward invisible unapproachable powers
of God; they can rise no higher, nor be anything else
in themselves, but as temples, habitations, or instru-

ments, in which the supernatural God can, and does manifest Himself in various degrees, bringing forth creatures to be good with His own goodness, to love and adore Him with His own spirit of love, for ever singing praises to the divine nature by that which they partake of it. This is the religion of divine inspiration, which, being interpreted, is Immanuel, or God within us. Everything short of this is short of that religion which worships God in spirit and in truth. And every religious trust or confidence in anything but the divine operation within us is but a sort of image-worship, which, though it may deny the form, yet retains the power thereof in the heart. And he that places any religious safety in theological decisions, scholastic points, in particular doctrines and opinions, that must be held about the Scripture words of faith, justification, sanctification, election, and reprobation, so far departs from the true worship of the living God within him, and sets up an idol of notions to be worshipped, if not instead of, yet along with Him. And I believe it may be taken for a certain truth, that every society of Christians whose religion stands upon this ground, however ardent, laborious, and good their zeal may seem to be in such matters, yet, in spite of all, sooner or later, it will be found that nature is at the bottom, and that a selfish, earthly, overbearing pride in their own definitions and doctrines of words will by degrees creep up to the same height, and become that same fleshly wisdom, doing those very same things, which they exclaim against in popes, cardinals, and Jesuits. Nor can it possibly be otherwise. For a letter-learned zeal has but one nature wherever it is; it can only do that for Christians

which it did for Jews. As it anciently brought forth
scribes, Pharisees, hypocrites, and crucifiers of Christ,
as it afterwards brought forth heresies, schisms, popes,
papal decrees, images, anathemas, transubstantiation,
so in Protestant countries it will be doing the same
thing, only with other materials ; images of wood and
clay, will only be given up for images of doctrines;
grace and works, imputed sin, and imputed righteousness, election, and reprobation will have their Synods
of Dort, as truly evangelical, as any Council of Trent.

15. Our Salvation only in the Life of Christ Jesus in us.

This must be the case of all fallen Christendom,
as well Popish as Protestant, till single men and
churches know, confess, and firmly adhere to this one
Scripture truth, which the blessed Behmen prefixed as
a motto to most of his epistles, namely, "That our
salvation is in the life of Jesus Christ in us." And
that, because this alone was the divine perfection of
man before he fell, and will be his perfection when he
is one with Christ in heaven. Everything besides
this, or that is not solely aiming at and essentially leading to it, is but mere Babel in all sects and divisions of
Christians, living to themselves, and their own old
man under a seeming holiness of Christian strife and
contention about Scripture works. But this truth of
truths, fully possessed, and firmly adhered to, brings
God and man together, puts an end to every Lo here
and Lo there, and turns the whole faith of man to a
Christ that can nowhere be a Saviour to him, but as
essentially born in the inmost spirit of his soul, nor

possible to be born there by any other means, but the
immediate inspiration and working power of the Holy
Spirit within him. To this man alone all Scripture
gives daily edification; the words of Christ and His
apostles fall like a fire into him. And what is it
that they kindle there? Not notions, not itching
ears, nor rambling desires after new and new ex-
pounders of them, but a holy frame of love, to be
always with, always attending to, that Christ and His
Holy Spirit within him, which alone can make him to
be and do all that, which the words of Christ and His
apostles have taught. For there is no possibility of
being like-minded with Christ in anything that He
taught, or having the truth of one Christian virtue,
but by the nature and Spirit of Christ become essentially living in us. Read all our Saviour's divine
sermon from the Mount, consent to the goodness of
every part of it, yet the time of practising it will
never come till you have a new nature from Christ,
and are as vitally in Him, and He in you, as the vine in
the branch, and the branch in the vine. "Blessed are
the pure in heart, for they shall see God," is a divine
truth, but will do us no divine good, unless we receive it
as saying neither more nor less, than "Blessed are they
that are born again of the Spirit, for they alone can
see God." For no blessedness, either of truth or life,
can be found either in men or angels, but where the
Spirit and Life of God is essentially born within them.

16. The Religion of Self or Nature.

And all men or churches, not placing all in the
life, light, and guidance of the Holy Spirit of Christ,

but pretending to act in the name, and for the glory
of God, from opinions which their logic and learning
have collected from Scripture words, or from what a
Calvin, an Arminius, a Socinus, or some smaller name,
has told them to be right or wrong, all such are but
where the apostles were, when " by the way there was
a strife among them who should be the greatest."
And how much soever they may say, and boast of
their great zeal for truth, and the only glory of God, yet
their own open notorious behaviour towards one another
is proof enough, that the great strife amongst them is,
which shall be the greatest sect or have the largest
number of followers. A strife, from the same root,
and just as useful to Christianity, as that of the carnal
apostles, who should be greatest. For not numbers of
men, or kingdoms professing Christianity, but numbers
redeemed from the death of Adam to the life of
Christ, are the glory of the Christian Church. And
in whatever national Christianity anything else is
meant or sought after, by the profession of the gospel,
but a new heavenly life, through the mediatorial
nature and spirit of the eternal Son of God, born in
the fallen soul, wherever this spirituality of the
gospel-redemption is denied or overlooked, there the
spirit of self, of satanic and worldly subtlety, will
be church and priest, and supreme power, in all that
is called religion.

But to return now to the doctrine of continual
inspiration. The natural or unregenerate man, educated in pagan learning and scholastic theology, seeing
the strength of his genius in the search after knowledge, how easily and learnedly he can talk and write,
criticise and determine upon all Scripture words and

facts, looks at all this as a full proof of his own religious wisdom, power, and goodness, and calls immediate inspiration enthusiasm, not considering that all the woes denounced by Christ against scribes, Pharisees, and hypocrites, are so many woes now at this day denounced against every appearance and show of religion, that the natural man can practise.

And what is well to be noted, everyone, however high in human literature, is but this very natural man, and can only have the goodness of a carnal secular religion, till as empty of all, as a new-born child, the Spirit of God gets a full birth in him, and becomes the inspirer and doer of all that he wills, does, and aims at in his whole course of religion.

Our Divine Master compares the religion of the learned Pharisees "to whited sepulchres, outwardly beautiful, but inwardly full of rottenness, stench, and dead men's bones."

Now whence was it, that a religion, so serious in its restraints, so beautiful in its outward form and practices, and commanding such reverence from all that beheld it, was yet charged by Truth itself with having inwardly such an abominable nature? It was only for this one reason, because it was a religion of self. Therefore, from the beginning to the end of the world, it must be true, that where self is kept alive, has power, and keeps up its own interests, whether in speaking, writing, teaching, or defending the most specious number of Scripture doctrines and religious forms, there is that very old Pharisee still alive, whom Christ with so much severity of language constantly condemned. And the reason of such heavy condemnation is, because self is the only root, or rather the

sum total of all sin; every sin that can be named is
centred in it, and the creature can sin no higher, than
he can live to self. For self is the fulness of atheism
and idolatry, it is nothing else but the creature broken
off from God and Christ; it is the power of Satan
living and working in us, and the sad continuance of
that first turning from God, which was the whole fall
or death of our first father.

And yet, sad and satanical as this self is, what is
so much cherished and nourished with our daily love,
fears, and cares about it? How much worldly wisdom,
how much laborious learning, how many subtleties of
contrivance, and how many flattering applications and
submissions are made to the world, that this apostate
self may have its fulness, both of inward joys and
outward glory?

But to all this it must yet be added, that a religion
of self, of worldly glory and prosperity carried on
under the gospel state, has more of a diabolical nature
than that of the Jewish Pharisees. It is the highest
and last working of the mystery of iniquity, because
it lives to self, Satan, and the world, in and by a daily
profession of denying and dying to self, of being
crucified with Christ, of being led by His Spirit, of
being risen from the world, and set with Him in
heavenly places.

Let then the writers against continual immediate
divine inspiration take this for a certain truth, that
by so doing, they do all they can to draw man from
that which is the very truth and perfection of the
gospel state, and are, and can be, no better than
pitiable advocates for a religion of self, more blamable
and abominable now, than that which was of old con-

demned by Christ. For whatever is pretended to be done in gospel religion by any other spirit or power, but that of the Holy Ghost bringing it forth, whether it be praying, preaching, or practising any duties, is all of it but the religion of self, and can be nothing else. For all that is born of the flesh, is flesh, and nothing is spiritual, but that which has its whole birth from the Spirit. But man, not ruled and governed by the Spirit, has only the nature of corrupt flesh, is under the full power and guidance of fallen nature, and is that very natural man to whom the things of God are foolishness. But man boldly rejecting, and preaching against a continual immediate divine inspiration, is an anti-apostle, he lays another foundation, than that which Christ has laid, he teaches that Christ needs not, must not, be all in all in us, and is a preacher up of the folly of fearing to grieve, quench, and resist the Holy Spirit.

17. Of Grieving and Resisting the Spirit.

For when, or where, or how could everyone of us be in danger of grieving, quenching, or resisting the Spirit, unless His holy breathings and inspirations were always within us? Or how could the sin against the Holy Ghost have a more dreadful nature, than that against the Father and the Son, but because the continual immediate guidance and operation of the Spirit, is the last and highest manifestation of the holy Trinity in the fallen soul of man? It is not because the Holy Ghost is more worthy, or higher in nature than the Father and the Son, but because Father and Son come forth in their own highest power of redeeming love, through the covenant of a continual immediate inspiration of the Spirit, to be always dwelling and working in the soul. Many weak things have been conjectured, and published to the world, about the sin against the Holy Ghost; whereas the whole nature of it lies in this, that it is a sinning or standing out against the last and highest dispensation of God for the full redemption of man. Christ says, "If I had not come, they had not had sin," that is, they had not had such a weight of guilt upon them; therefore the sinning against Christ come into the flesh, was of a more unpardonable nature, than sinning against the Father under the law. So likewise sinning against the Holy Ghost is of a more unpardonable nature than sinning against the Father under the law, or against the Son as come in the flesh, because these two preceding dispensations were but preparatory to the coming, or full ministration of the Spirit. But when Father and Son were come in the power and manifestation of the Spirit, then he that refuses or resists this ministration of the Spirit, resists all that the holy Trinity can do to restore and revive the first life of God in the soul, and so commits the unpardonable sin, and which is therefore unpardonable, because there remains no further, or higher power to remove it out of the soul. For no sin is pardonable, because of its own nature, or that which it is in itself, but because there is something yet to come that can remove it out of the soul; nor can any sin be unpardonable, but because it has withstood or turned from that which was the last and highest remedy for the removal of it.

Hence it is, that grieving, quenching, or resisting

the Spirit, is the sin of all sins, that most of all stops the work of redemption, and in the highest degree separates man from all union with God. But there could be no such sin, but because the Holy Spirit is always breathing, willing, and working within us. For what spirit can be grieved by us, but that which has its will within us disobeyed? What spirit can be quenched by us, but that which is, and ever would be, a holy fire of life within us? What spirit can be resisted by us, but that which is, and has its working within us? A spirit on the outside of us cannot be the Spirit of God, nor could such a spirit be any more quenched, or hindered by our spirit, than a man by indignation at a storm could stop its rage. Now, dreadful as the above-mentioned sin is, I would ask all the writers against continual immediate divine inspiration, how they could more effectually lead men into an habitual state of sinning against the Holy Ghost, than by such doctrine? For how can we possibly avoid the sin of grieving, quenching, etc., the Spirit, but by continually reverencing His holy presence in us, by continually waiting for, trusting, and solely attending to that which the Spirit of God wills, works, and manifests within us? To turn men from this continual dependence upon the Holy Spirit, is turning them from all true knowledge of God. For without this, there is no possibility of any edifying, saving knowledge of God. For though we have ever so many mathematical demonstrations of His Being, etc., we are without all real knowledge of Him, till His own quickening Spirit within us manifests Him, as a power of life, light, love, and goodness, essentially found, vitally felt, and adored in our souls. This is the one knowledge of God, which is eternal life, because it is the life of God manifested in the soul, that knowledge of which Christ says, "No one knoweth the Father but the Son, and He to whomsoever the Son revealeth Him." Therefore this knowledge is only possible to be found in Him, who is in Christ a new creature, for so it is that Christ revealeth the Father. But if none belong to God, but those who are led by the Spirit of God, if we are reprobates unless the Spirit of Christ be living in us, who need be told, that all we have to trust to or depend upon, as children of God and Christ, is the continual immediate guidance, unction, and teaching of His Holy Spirit within us? Or how can we more profanely sin against this Spirit and power of God within us, or more expressly call men from the power of God to Satan, than by ridiculing a faith and hope that look wholly and solely to His continual immediate breathings and operations, for all that can be holy and good in us?

"When I am lifted up from the earth," says Christ, "I will draw all men unto Me." Therefore the one great power of Christ in and over the souls of men is after He is in heaven; then begins the true full power of His drawing, because it is by His Spirit in man that He draws. But who can more resist this drawing, or defeat its operation in us, than he that preaches against, and condemns the belief of a continual and immediate inspiration of the Spirit, when Christ's drawing can be in nothing else, nor be powerful any other way?

18. All Scripture teaches us our entire dependence upon the Spirit of God.

Now, that which we are here taught, is the whole end of all Scripture; for all that is there said, however learnedly read, or studied by Hebrew or Greek skill, fails of its only end, till it leads and brings us to an essential God within us, to feel and find all that which the Scriptures speak of God, of man, of life and death, of good and evil, of heaven and hell, as essentially verified in our own souls. For all is within man that can be either good or evil to him; God within him, is his divine life, his divine light, and his divine love; Satan within him is his life of self, of earthly wisdom, of diabolical falseness, wrath, pride, and vanity of every kind. There is no middle way between these two. He that is not under the power of the one, is under the power of the other. And the reason is, man was created in and under the power of the divine life; so far therefore as he loses, or turns from this life of God, so far he falls under the power of self, of Satan, and worldly wisdom. When St. Peter, full of an human good love towards Christ, advised him to avoid his sufferings, Christ rejected him with a "Get thee behind Me, Satan," and only gave this reason for it, "for thou savourest not the things that be of God, but the things that be of men." A plain proof, that whatever is not of and from the Holy Spirit of God in us, however plausible it may outwardly seem to men, to their wisdom, and human goodness, is yet in itself nothing else but the power of Satan in us. And as St. Paul said truly of himself, "by the grace of God I am what I am"; so every wise, every scribe, every

disputer of this world, every truster to the strength of
his own rational learning, everyone that is under the
power of his own fallen nature, never free from desires
of honours and preferments, ever thirsting to be
rewarded for his theological abilities, ever fearing to
be abased and despised, always thankful to those who
flatter him with his distinguished merit, everyone that
is such, be he who he will, may as truly say of himself,
Through my turning and trusting to something else
than the grace and inspiration of God's Spirit, I am
what I am. For nothing else hinders any professor
of Christ from being able truly to say with St. Paul,
"God forbid that I should glory in anything but the
cross of Christ, by which I am crucified to the world,
and the world to me." Nothing makes him incapable
of finding that which St. Paul found, when he said,
"I can do all things through Christ that strengtheneth
me"; nothing hinders all this, but his disregard of a
Christ within him, his choosing to have a religion of
self, of laborious learning, and worldly greatness,
rather than be such a gospel fool for Christ, as to
renounce all that which He renounced, and to seek no
more earthly honour and praise than He did, and to
will nothing, know nothing, seek nothing, but that
which the Spirit of God and Christ knows, wills, and
seeks in Him. Here, and here alone, lies the Christian's full and certain power of overcoming self, the
devil, and the world. But Christians, seeking and
turning to anything else, but to be led and inspired
by the one Spirit of God and Christ, will bring forth
a Christendom that in the sight of God will have no
other name, than a spiritual Babylon, a spiritual
Egypt, and Sodom, a scarlet whore, a devouring beast,

and red dragon. For all these names belong to all
men, however learned, and to all churches, whether
greater or less, in which the spirit of this world has
any share of power.   This was the fall of the whole
Church soon after the apostolic ages; and all human
reformations, begun by ecclesiastical learning, and
supported by civil power, will signify little or nothing,
nay often make things worse, till all churches, dying
to all own will, all own wisdom, all own advancement,
seek for no reforming power but from that Spirit of
God which converted sinners, publicans, harlots, Jews,
and heathens, into an holy apostolical church at the
first, a church which knew they were of God, that
they belonged to God, by that Spirit which He had
given them, and which worked in them.

"Ye are not in the flesh," says the apostle, "but in
the Spirit"; but then he adds, as the only ground of
this, "If so be that the Spirit of God dwelleth in
you"; surely he means if so be ye are moved, guided,
and governed by that, which the Spirit wills, works,
and inspires within you.   And then to show the
absolute necessity of this life of God in the soul, he
adds, "If any man hath not the Spirit of Christ, he is
none of His."   And that this is the state to which
God has appointed, and called all Christians, he thus
declares, "God hath sent forth the Spirit of His Son
into your hearts, crying, Abba, Father" (Gal. iv. 6).
The same thing, most surely, as if he had said,
nothing in you can cry, or pray to God as its
Father, but the Spirit of His Son Christ come to life
in you.   Which is also as true of every tendency in
the soul towards God or goodness; so much as there
is of it, so much there is of the seed of the woman

striving to bring forth a full birth of Christ in the soul.

19. Of Christ's Coming into our Hearts as a Living, Holy Nature within us.

"Lo, I am always with you," says the holy Jesus, "even to the end of the world." How is he with us? Not outwardly, every illiterate man knows; not inwardly, says many a learned doctor, because a Christ within us is as gross enthusiasm, or Quakerism, as the light within us. How then shall the faith of the common Christian find any comfort in these words of Christ's promise, unless the Spirit brings him into a remembrance and belief, that Christ is in him, and with him, as the vine is with and in the branch. Christ says, "Without Me ye can do nothing"; and also, "If any man loves Me, My Father will love him, and we will come unto him, and make our abode with him." Now if without Him we can do nothing, then all the love that a man can possibly have for Christ, must be from the power and life of Christ in him, and from such a love, so begotten, man has the Father and the Son dwelling and making their abode in him. What higher proof, or fuller certainty can there be, that the whole work of redemption in the soul of man is and can be nothing else, but the inward, continual, immediate operation of Father, Son, and Holy Spirit, raising up again their own first life in the soul, to which our first father died?

Again, Christ, after His glorification in Heaven, says, "Behold **I stand** at the **door** and knock." He does not say, Behold ye have Me in the Scriptures.

Now what is the door at which Christ, at the right hand of God in Heaven, knocks? Surely it is the heart, to which Christ is always present. He goes on, "If any man hear My voice"; how hears, but by the hearing of the heart, or what voice, but that which is the speaking or sounding of Christ within him; He adds, "and opens the door," that is, opens his heart for Me, "I will come in to him," that is, will be a living holy nature, and spirit born within him, "and sup with him, and he with Me." Behold the last finishing work of a redeeming Jesus, entered into the heart that opens to Him, bringing forth the joy, the blessing, and perfection of that first life of God in the soul, which was lost by the Fall, set forth as a supper, or feast of the heavenly Jesus with the soul, and the soul with Him. Can anyone justly call it enthusiasm to say, that this supping of the soul with this glorified Christ within it, must mean something more heavenly transacted in the soul than that last supper which He celebrated with His disciples, whilst He was with them in flesh. For that supper of bread and wine was such, as a Judas could partake of, and could only be an outward type or signification of that inward and blessed nourishment, with which the believing soul should be feasted, when the glorified Son of God should as a creating spirit enter into us, quickening, and raising up His own heavenly nature and life within us. Now this continual knocking of Christ at the door of the heart, sets forth the case or nature of a continual immediate divine inspiration within us; it is always with us, but there must be an opening of the heart to it; and though it is always there, yet it is only felt and found by those, who are attentive to it, depend

upon, and humbly wait for it. Now let anyone tell
me how he can believe anything of this voice of
Christ, how he can listen to it, hear, or obey it, but by
such a faith, as keeps him habitually turned to an
immediate constant inspiration of the Spirit of Christ
within him? Or how any heathenish profane person
can do more despite to this presence and power of
Christ in his own soul, or more effectually lead others
into it, than that ecclesiastic, who makes a mock at the
light within, a Christ within, and openly blasphemes
that faith, and hope, and trust, which solely relies
upon being moved by the Spirit, as its only power of
doing that which is right, and good, and pious either
towards God or man. Let every man, whom this
concerns, lay it to heart. Time, and the things of
time, will soon have an end; and he that in time
trusts to anything but the Spirit and power of God
working in his heart, will be ill-fitted to enter into
eternity; God must be all and all in us here, or we
cannot be His hereafter. Time works only for
eternity; and poverty eternal must as certainly follow
him, who dies only fully stuffed with human learning,
as he who dies only full of worldly riches. The folly
of thinking to have any divine learning, but that
which the Holy Spirit teaches, or to make ourselves
rich in knowledge towards God, by heaps of commonplace learning crowded into our minds, will leave us
as dreadfully cheated as that rich builder of barns in
the gospel, to whom it was said, "Thou fool, this
night shall thy soul be required of thee. And then,
whose shall all these things be?" (Luke xii.). So is
every man that treasures up a religious learning that
comes not wholly from the Spirit of God.

20. Both God and Satan have their work within us.

But to return. To this inward continual attention to the continual working of the Holy Spirit
within us, the apostle calls us in these words, " See
that ye refuse not Him that speaketh ; for if they
escaped not who refused Him that spoke on earth,
much more shall not we escape, if we turn from Him
that speaketh from Heaven " (Heb. xii. 25). Now
what is this speaking from heaven which it is so
dangerous to refuse or resist ? Surely not outward
voices from heaven. Or what could the apostle's
advice signify to us, unless it be such a speaking from
heaven, as we may and must be always either obeying
or refusing ? St. James saith, " Resist the devil, and
he will flee from you." What devil ? Surely not an
outward creature or spirit, that tempts us by an
outward power. Or what resistance can we make to
the devil, but that of inwardly falling away, or turning
from the workings of his evil nature and spirit within
us ? They therefore who call us from waiting for,
depending upon, and attending to the continual secret
inspirations and breathings of the Holy Spirit within
us, call us to resist God in the same manner as the
apostle exhorts us to resist the devil. For God being
only a spiritual good, and the devil our spiritual evil,
neither the one nor the other can be resisted, or not
resisted by us, but so far as their spiritual operations
within us are either turned from or obeyed by us.
St. James having shown us that resisting the devil is
the only way to make him flee from us, that is, to
lose his power in us, immediately adds, how we are to

behave towards God, that He may not flee from us, or
His holy work be stopped in us. " Draw near," saith
he, " to God, and God will draw near to you." What
is this drawing near? Surely not by any local
motion either in God or us. But the same is meant,
as if he had said, resist not God, that is, let His holy
will within you have its full work; keep wholly,
obediently attentive to that, which He is, and has, and
does within you, and then God will draw near to you,
that is, will more and more manifest the power of His
holy presence in you, and make you more and more
partakers of the divine nature.

21. The Teaching of the Church on Continual Inspiration.

Further, what a blindness is it in the forementioned
writers, to charge private persons with the enthusiasm
of holding the necessity, and certainty of continual
immediate inspiration, and to attack them as enemies
to the Established Church, when everybody's eyes see,
that collect after collect, in the Established Liturgy,
teaches and requires them to believe, and pray for the
continual inspiration of the Spirit, as that alone, by
which they can have the least good thought or desire?
Thus," O God, forasmuch as without Thee we are not able
to please Thee, mercifully grant that Thy Holy Spirit
may in all things direct and rule our hearts." Is it
possible for words more strongly to express the necessity
of a continual divine inspiration? Or can inspiration
be higher, or more immediate in prophets and apostles,
than that which directs, that which rules our hearts,
not now and then, but in all things? Or can the

absolute necessity of this be more fully declared, than
by saying, that if it is not in this degree both of
height and continuance in and over our hearts, nothing
that is done by us can be pleasing to God, that is, can
have any union with Him.

Now the matter is not at all about the different effects
or works proceeding from inspiration, as whether by it
a man be made a saint in himself, or sent by God with
a prophetic message to others, this affects not the
nature and necessity of inspiration, which is just as
great, just as necessary in itself to all true goodness,
as to all true prophecy. All Scripture is of divine
inspiration. But why so? " Because holy men of
old spoke as they were moved by the Holy Ghost."
Now the above collect, as well as Christ and His
apostles oblige us in like manner to hold, that all
holiness is by divine inspiration, and that therefore
there could have been no holy men of old, or in any
latter times, but solely for this reason, because " they
lived as they were moved by the Holy Ghost." Again,
the liturgy prays thus, " O God, from whom all good
things do come, grant that by Thy holy inspiration we
may think those things that be good, and by Thy
merciful guiding may perform the same." Now, if in
any of my writings I have ever said anything higher,
or further of the nature and necessity of continual
divine inspiration, than this Church prayer does, I
refuse no censure that shall be passed upon me. But
if I have, from all that we know of God, of nature,
and creature, shown the utter impossibility of any
kind, or degree of goodness to be in us, but from the
divine nature living and breathing in us, if I have
shown that all Scripture, Christ and his apostles, over

and over say the same thing; that our Church liturgy
is daily praying according to it; what kinder thing
can I say of those Churchmen who accuse me of
enthusiasm, than that which Christ said of his blind
crucifiers, "Father, forgive them, for they know not
what they do."

22. Of the Abuse of the Doctrine by Enthusiasts.

It is to no purpose to object to all this, that these
kingdoms are overrun with enthusiasts of all kinds,
and that Moravians with their several divisions, and
Methodists of various kinds, are everywhere acting in
the wildest manner, under the pretence of being called
and led by the Spirit.   Be it so, or not so, is a matter
I meddle not with ; nor is the doctrine I am upon in
the least affected by it.   For what an argument would
this be; enthusiasts of the present and former ages
have made a bad use of the doctrine of being led by
the Spirit of God, *ergo*, " He is enthusiastic, or helps
forward enthusiasm, who preaches up the doctrine of
being led by the Spirit of God."   Now, absurd as this
is, was any of my accusers as high in genius, as bulky
in learning, as Colossus was in stature, he would be at
a loss to bring a stronger argument than this to prove
me an enthusiast, or an abettor of them.

But as I do not begin to doubt about the necessity,
the truth, and perfection of gospel religion, when told
that whole nations and churches have, under a pretence of regard to it, and for the sake of it, done all
the bad things that can be charged upon this or that
leading enthusiast, whether you call those bad things,

schism, perjury, rebellion, worldly craft, and hypocrisy, etc. So I give not up the necessity, the truth, and perfection of looking wholly to the Spirit of God and Christ within me, as my promised inspirer and only worker of all that can be good in me; I give not this up, because in this, or that age, both spiritual pride and fleshly lusts have prospered by it, or because Satan has often led people into all the heights of self-glory, and self-seeking, under a pretence of being inspired with gospel humility, and gospel self-denial.

23. Of Denying our Reason in Religion as an essential part of Self-denial.

Another charge upon me, equally false, and, I may say, more senseless, is that I am a declared enemy to the use of reason in religion. And why? Because in all my writings, I teach that reason is to be denied, etc. I own, I have not only taught this, but have again and again proved the absolute necessity of it. And this, because Christ has made it absolutely necessary by saying, "Whosoever will come after Me, let him deny himself," etc. For how can a man deny himself, without denying his reason, unless reason be no part of himself? Or how can a rational creature, whose chief distinction from brutes is that of his reason, be called to deny himself any other way, than by denying that which is peculiar to himself? Let the matter be thus expressed, Man is not to deny his reason. Well, how then? Why (N.B.), he is only to deny himself. Can there be a greater folly of words? And yet it is their wisdom of words, who allow the denying of self to be good doctrine, but boggle, and cry out at the denying of reason, as quite bad. For how can a man deny himself, but by denying that which is the life, and spirit, and power of self? What makes a man a sinner? Nothing but the power and working of his natural reason. And, therefore, if our natural reason is not to be denied, we must keep up and follow that which works every sin that ever was, or can be in us. For we can sin nowhere, or in anything, but where our natural reason or understanding has its power in us. What is meant in all Scripture by the flesh and its works? Is it something distinct and different from the workings of our rational and intelligent nature? No, it is our whole intelligent, rational nature that constitutes the flesh on the carnal man, who could not be criminally so, any more than the beasts, but because his carnality has all its evil from his intelligent nature or reason, being the life and power of it. And everything which our Lord says of self, is so much said of our natural reason; and all that the Scripture says of the flesh and its evil nature, is so much said of the evil state of our natural reason, which therefore is, ought, and must be denied, in the same manner and degree as self and flesh is, and must be denied.

I have elsewhere shown the gross darkness and ignorance which govern that which is called metaphysics in the schools, "that it is so great, that if you were to say, that God first creates a soul out of nothing, and when that is done, then takes an understanding faculty and puts it into it, after that, adds a will, and then a memory, all as independently made, as when a tailor first makes the body of a coat, and then adds sleeves and pockets to it; were you to say this, the schools of Descartes, Malebranche, or Locke, could have nothing to say against it."[1]

And here truth obliges me to say that scholastic divinity is in as great ignorance about the most fundamental truths of the gospel, as I have again and again shown, in regard to the nature of the fall of man, and all the Scripture expressions concerning the new birth; and here also concerning the doctrine of a man's denying himself, which modern learning supposes to be possible without, or different from a man's denying his own natural reason; which is an absurdity of the greatest magnitude. For what is self, but that which a man is, and has in his natural capacity? Or what is the fulness of his natural capacity, but the strength and power of his reason? How then can any man deny himself, but by denying that which gives self its whole nature, name, and power? If man was not a rational creature, he could not be called to deny himself, he could not need or receive the benefit and goodness of self-denial: no man, therefore, can obey the precept of denying himself, or have any benefit or goodness from it, but so far as he denies, or dies to his own natural reason, because the self of man, and the natural reason of man, are strictly the same thing. Again, our Blessed Lord said in His agony, " Not My will, but Thine be done." And had not this been the form of His whole life, He had not lived without sin. Now, thus to deny our own will that God's will may be done in us, is the height of our calling; and so far as we keep from our

[1] *Spirit of Love*, First Part.

own natural will, so far we keep from sin. But now, if our own natural will, as having all sin and evil in it, is always to be denied, whatever it costs us, I would fain know how our natural reason can ever escape, or how we can deny our own will, and not deny that rational or intelligent power, in and from which the will has its whole existence and continual direction ? Or how there can be always a badness of our own will, which is not the badness of our own natural intellectual power ? Therefore, it is a truth of the utmost certainty, that as much as we are obliged to deny our own natural will that the will of God may be done in us, so much are we obliged to deny our own natural reason and understanding that our own will may not be done or followed by us. For whoever lives to his own natural reason, he necessarily lives to his own natural will. For our natural will, in whatever state it is, is nothing else but our natural reason willing this, or that.

Now, hard as this may seem to unregenerate nature, and yet harder to nature highly exalted, and big with the glory of all that which wits, poets, orators, critics, sophists, and historians have enriched it with, yet true it is, and a truth as certain as the fall of man, that this full denial of our own natural will, and our own natural reason, is the only possible way for divine knowledge, divine light, and divine goodness, to have any place or power of birth in us. All other religious knowledge got any other way, let it be as great as it will, is only great in vanity, emptiness, and delusion. For nothing but that which comes immediately from God can have anything godly in it, and all that which comes from self, and natural reason, however outwardly coloured, can have no better a nature within than self-seeking, self-esteem, and fleshly wisdom, which (N.B.) are those very works of the devil in us, which Christ came into the world to destroy. For the efforts of natural reason, and self-abilities, to be great in religious knowledge from our own particular talents, are as satanical things as any we carry about us, and most of all fix us in the highest contrariety to that state, which our Lord affirms to be absolutely necessary.

"Except ye be converted, and become as little children, ye cannot enter into the kingdom of God." Now, as sure as this is necessary, so sure is it, that no one can be thus converted or come under the good influence of this childlike nature, till natural reason, self, and own will are all equally denied. For all the evil and corruption of our fallen nature consists in this, it is an awakened life of own reason, own will broken off from God, and so fallen into the selfish workings of its own earthly nature.

Now, whether this self broken off from God, reasons, wills, and contends about the difference of Scripture words and opinions, or reasons against them all, the same evil state of fallen nature, the same loss of life, the same separation from God, the same evil tempers of flesh and blood, will be equally strengthened and inflamed by the one as by the other,—hence it is that Papists and Protestants are hating, fighting, and killing one another for the sake of their different excellent opinions, and yet, as to the lusts of the flesh, the lust of the eye, and the pride of life, they are in the highest union and communion with one another. For if you expect a zealous Protestant to be therefore

a new-born creature alive unto God, or a zealous
Papist to be therefore dead to all divine goodness, you
may be said to have lived in the world without either
eyes or ears. And the reason why it must be so, is
because bad syllogisms for transubstantiation, and
better syllogisms against it, signify no more towards
the casting Satan out of our souls, than a bad or
better taste for painting.

Hence also it is, that Christendom, full of the nicest
decisions about faith, grace, works, merits, satisfaction,
heresies, schisms, etc., is full of all those evil tempers
which prevailed in the heathen world, when none of
these things were ever thought of.

A scholar, pitying the blindness and folly of those
who live to themselves in the cares and pleasures of
this vain life, thinks himself divinely employed, and
to have escaped the pollutions of the world, because
he is, day after day, dividing, dissecting, and mending
church opinions, fixing heresies here, schisms there;
forgetting all the while that a carnal self and natural
reason have the doing of all that is done by this
learned zeal, and are as busy and active in him as in
the reasoning infidel or projecting worldling. For
where self is wholly denied, there nothing can be
called heresy, schism, or wickedness, but the want of
loving God with our whole heart, and our neighbour
as ourselves; nor anything be called truth, life, or
salvation, but the spirit, nature, and power of Christ
living and manifesting itself in us as it did in Him.
But where self or the natural man is become great in
religious learning, there the greater the scholar, the
more firmly will he be fixed in their religion, whose
God is their belly. I write not to reason, says the

blessed Jacob Behmen; Oh, enthusiasm! says the
Mouth of Learning: and yet Jacob said as sober a truth
as if he had said, I write not to self and own will; for
natural reason, self and own will always did, and
always must see through the same eyes, and hear
through the same ears. Now, let it only be supposed
that Behmen and myself, when we speak of natural
reason, mean only the natural man (as is over and over
declared by us), and then Behmen's saying, that he
writes neither from reason nor to the natural reason
of others, is only saying that very same thing as St.
Paul says, that "the natural man receiveth not the
things of the Spirit of God, for they are foolishness
unto him (N.B.), neither can he know them (N.B.),
because they are spiritually discerned."

24. The Use of Reason in Religion.

But that I may fully show the perverseness of my
accusers in charging me with denying the use of
reason in religion, see here a word or two of what I
have said at large, and in the plainest words, more
than twenty-four years ago, which doctrine I have
maintained in all that I have since wrote. My words
are these :—

"You shall see reason possessed of all that belongs
to it. I will grant it to have as great a share in the
good things of religion, as in the good things of this
life; that it can assist the soul, just as it can assist
the body, that it has the same power and virtue in
the spiritual, that it has in the natural world; that it
can communicate to us as much of the one, as of the
other, and is of the same use and importance in the

one as in the other. Can you ask more?" All
which I thus make out in the following manner:—

"Man, considered as a member of this world, who
is to have his share of the good that is in it, is a
sensible and a rational creature, that is, he has a
certain number of senses, as seeing, hearing, tasting,
touching, and smelling, by which he is sensible of that
which the outward world, in which he is placed, can
do for him, or communicate to him, and so is sensible
of what kind and degree of happiness he can have
from it.

"Now, besides these organs of sense, he has a
power or faculty of reasoning upon the ideas which
he has received from these senses.

"Now, how is it that the good things of this world
are communicated to man? How is he put in possession of them? To what part of him are they pro-
posed? Are his senses, or his reason, the means of
his having so much as he has or can have from this
world?

"Now here, you must degrade reason just as much
as it is degraded by religion, and are obliged to set it
as low with respect to the things of this world, as it is
set with respect to the things of the spiritual world.
It is no more the means of communicating the good
things of the one, than of the other. And as St. Paul
says, 'The natural man cannot receive the things of
the Spirit of God,' for this reason, because they are
spiritually discerned; so you must of necessity say,
the rational man cannot receive the things of this
world, for this reason, because they are sensibly
received, that is, by the organs of sense. Reason
therefore has no higher office or power in the things

of this world, than in the things of religion; and
religion does no more violence to your reason, or
rejects it in any other way, than all the good things of
this world reject it; it is not seeing, it is not hearing,
tasting, or feeling the things of this life; it can supply
the place of no one of these senses.

"Now it is only thus helpless and useless in religion; it is neither seeing, nor hearing, tasting, nor
feeling of spiritual things; therefore in the things of
religion, and in the things of this world, it has one
and the same insignificance. It is the sensibility of
the soul that must receive what this world can communicate to it; it is the sensibility of the soul that
must receive what God can communicate: reason may
follow after in either case, and view through its own
glass what is done, but it can do no more. Reason
may be here of the same service to us, as when we
want any of the enjoyments of this life; it may direct
us how and where they are to be had; it may take
away a cover from our eyes, or open our window-
shutters when we want the light: but it can do no
more towards seeing, than to make way for the light
to act upon our eyes. This is all its office and ability
in the things of religion; it may remove that which
hinders the sensibility of the soul, or prevents the
divine light's acting upon it, but it can do no more;
because the faculty of reasoning is only the activity
of the mind upon its own ideas or images, which the
senses have caused it to form from that which has
been stirred up in them, but has nothing of the nature
of that which it speculates upon by ideas; it does not
become dark, when it reasons upon the cause or nature
of darkness, nor becomes light, when it reasons about

it; neither is it religion, nor gets anything of the nature of religion, when it is wholly taken up in descriptions and definitions of religious doctrines and virtues.

"For the good of religion is like the good of food and drink to the creature that wants it.   And if instead of giving such an one bread and wine, you should teach him to seek for relief by attending to clear ideas of the nature of bread, of different ways of making it, etc., he would be left to die in the want of sustenance, just as the religion of reasoning leaves the soul to perish in the want of that good which it was to have from religion.   And yet as a man may have the benefit of food much assisted by the right use of his reason, though reason has not the good of food in it, so a man may have the good of religion much assisted and secured to him by the right use of his reason, though reason has not the good of religion in it. And as it would be great folly and perverseness to accuse a man as an enemy to the true use of reasoning about food, because he declares that reason is not food, nor can supply the place of it, so is it equally such to accuse a man as an enemy to the use of reasoning in religion, because he declares that reasoning is not religion, nor can supply the place of it.   We have no want of religion, but because we want to have more of the divine nature in us than we have in our fallen nature.   But if this be the truth of the matter (and who can deny it?), then we are sure that nothing can be our good in religion, but that which communicates to us something of God, or which alters our state of existence in God, and makes us partakers of the divine nature in such a manner and degree as we wanted.

What a folly is it then to put any trust in a religion of rational notions and opinions logically deduced from Scripture words? Do we not see sinners of all sorts, and men under the power of every corrupt passion, equally zealous for such a religion? Proof enough, that it has not the good of religion in it, nor any contrariety to the vices of the heart; it neither kills them, nor is killed by them. For as pride, hypocrisy, envy, or malice do not take away from the mind its geometrical or critical abilities; so a man may be most logical in his religion of reason, words, doctrines, and opinions, when he has nothing of the true good of religion in him.

"But as soon as it is known and confessed that all the happiness or misery of all creatures consists only in this, as they are more or less possessed of God, or as they differently partake of the divine nature, then it must be equally known, that nothing but God can do or be any religious good to us, and also that God cannot do, or be any religious good to us, but by the communication of Himself, or the manifestation of His own life within us."

Hence may be seen the great and like blindness both of infidels and Christians; the one in trusting to their own reason dwelling in its own logical conclusions; the other in trusting to their own reason dwelling in learned opinions about Scripture words and phrases, and doctrines built upon them. "For as soon as it is known and confessed that God is all in all, that in Him we live and move and have our being, that we can have nothing separately, or out of Him, but everything in Him, that we have no being or degree of being but in Him, that He can give us

nothing as our good but Himself, nor any degree of
salvation from our fallen nature, but in such degree
as He again communicates something more of Himself
to us, as soon as this is known, then it is known with
the utmost evidence, that to put a religious trust in
our own reason, whether confined to itself or working
in doctrines about Scripture words, has the nature of
that same idolatry that puts a religious trust in the
sun, a departed saint, or a graven image." [1]   And as
image-worship has often boasted of its divine power,
because of the wonders of zeal and devotion that have
been raised thereby in thousands and ten thousands of
its followers, so it is no marvel, if opinion-worship
should often have and boast of the same effects.   But
the truth of the whole matter lies here: as the word
manifested in the flesh or become man, is the one
Mediator or restorer of union between God and man,
so to seeing eyes it must be evident, that nothing but
this one mediatorial nature of Christ, essentially
brought to life in our souls, can be our salvation
through Christ Jesus.   For that which saved and
exalted that humanity in which Christ dwelt, must be
the salvation of every human creature in the world.

25. The Presence of the Holy Spirit means more than the Inspiration of the Holy Scriptures.

But to return.   What poor divinity knowledge
comes from great scholars, and great readers, may be
sufficiently seen from the two following judicious
quotations in a late dissertation on enthusiasm; the

[1] *Demonstration of the Gross Errors in the Plain Account, etc.*

one is taken from Dr. Warburton's sermons, the other from a pastoral letter of Mr. Stinstra, a preacher among the Mennonists of Friesland. That from Dr. Warburton stands thus: "By them (that is, by the writings of the New Testament) the prophetic promise of our Saviour, that the Comforter should abide for ever, was eminently fulfilled. For though His ordinary influence occasionally assists the faithful, yet His constant abode and supreme illumination is in the sacred Scriptures."[1] Dr. Warburton's doctrine is this, that the inspired books of the New Testament is that Comforter, or Spirit of Truth, and illuminator, which is meant by Christ's being always with His Church. Let us therefore put the Doctor's doctrine into the letter of the text, which will best show how true or false it is.

Our Lord says, 'It is expedient for you that I go away, or the Comforter will not come"; that is, it is expedient for you, that I leave off teaching you in words, that sound only into your outward ears, that you may have the same words in writing, for your outward eyes to look upon, for if I do not depart from this vocal way of teaching you, the Comforter will not come, that is, ye will not have the comfort of My words written on paper. But if I go away, I will send written books, which shall lead you into such a truth of words as you could not have, whilst they were only spoken from My mouth; but being written on paper, they will be My spiritual, heavenly, constant abode with you, and the most supreme illumination you can receive from Me.

Christ says further: " I have many things to say

[1] *Dissertation*, p. 10.

unto you, but ye cannot bear them now; howbeit when He, the Spirit of Truth, is come, He shall guide you into all truth; for He shall not speak of Himself, for He shall receive of Mine, and shall show it unto you;" that is, though you cannot be sufficiently instructed from My words at present, yet when they shall hereafter come to you in written books, they will give you a knowledge of all truth, for they shall not speak of themselves, but shall receive words from Me, and show them unto you. Again, Christ says, "These things have I spoken unto you in proverbs; but the time cometh, when I shall no more speak unto you in proverbs, but will show you plainly of the Father." That is, hitherto you have only had spoken proverbs from Me, and therefore you have not plainly known the Father; but the time cometh when these spoken proverbs shall be put into writing, and then you shall plainly know the Father. Again, Christ adds: "Ye now therefore have sorrow, but I will see you again, and your hearts shall rejoice, and your joy no man taketh from you." That is, you are now troubled at My personal departure from you, but some written books shall be My seeing you again, and in that visit you shall have such joy as cannot be taken from you.

Christ also says, "If any man loves Me, My Father will love him, and we will come unto him, and make our abode with him." That is, according to the Doctor's theology, certain books of Scripture will come to him, and make their abode with him; for he expressly confines the constant abode and supreme illumination of God to the Holy Scriptures. Therefore (horrible to say) God's inward presence, His

operating power of life and light in our souls, His
dwelling in us, and we in Him, is something of a
lower nature, that only may occasionally happen, and
has less of God in it than the dead letter of Scripture,
which alone is His constant abode and supreme illumination.   Miserable fruits of a paradoxical genius!

Christ from heaven says, "Behold I stand at the
door, and knock; if any man hear My voice, and
open unto Me, I will come into him, and sup with
him."   This is His true eminent fulfilling of His
prophetic promise of being a Comforter and Spirit of
Truth to His Church to the end of the world.   But
according to the Doctor, we are to understand, that
not the heavenly Christ but the New Testament continually stands and knocks at the door, wanting to
enter into the heart, and sup with it; which is no
better than holding, that when Christ calls Himself
Alpha and Omega, He means not Himself, but the
New Testament.   Again, "I am the vine, ye are the
branches; as the branch cannot bear fruit of itself,
except it abide in the vine, no more can ye,
except ye abide in Me; for without Me, ye can do
nothing."   Now take the Doctor's comment, and then
the truth of all these words of Christ was only tem-
porary, and could be true no longer, than till the books
of the New Testament were written; for then all this,
which Christ has affirmed of Himself, of the certainty
and necessity of His life and power in them, ended
in Christ, and passed over to the written words of the
New Testament, and they are the true vine, and we
its branches, they are that without which we can do
nothing.   For this it must be, if, as the Doctor affirms,
the writings of the New Testament are that, by which

we are to understand the constant abode and supreme illumination of God in man. Now absurd, and even blasphemous, as this interpretation of the foregoing text is, it must be evident to every reader, that it is all the Doctor's own; for the letter of Scripture is only made here to claim that divinity to itself, which the Doctor has openly affirmed to be true of it.

26. The true value of Scripture as an outward Guide to God's inward Teaching.

" Rabbi," says Nicodemus to Christ, " we know that Thou art a Teacher come from God." Now that which was here truly said of Christ in the flesh, is the very truth that must be said of the Scripture teaching in ink and paper; it is a teacher come from God, and therefore fully to be believed, highly reverenced, and strictly followed. But as Christ's teaching in the flesh was only preparatory to His future vital teaching by the Spirit, so the teaching of Scripture by words written with ink and paper is only preparatory, or introductory to all that inward essential teaching of God, which is by His Spirit and truth within us. Every other opinion of the Holy Scripture, but that of an outward teacher and guide to God's inward teaching and illumination in our souls, is but making an idol-god of it: I say an idol-god; for to those who rest in it as the constant abode and supreme illumination of God with them, it can be nothing else. For if nothing of divine faith, love, hope, or goodness, can have the least birth or place in us, but by divine inspiration, they who think these virtues may be sufficiently raised in us by the letter of Scripture, do in truth and reality make the letter of Scripture their inspiring God. The apostles preached and wrote to the people by divine inspiration. But what do they say of their inspired doctrine and teachings? What virtue or power was there in them? Do they say that their words and teachings were the very promised Comforter, the Spirit of Truth, the true abode and supreme illumination of God in the souls of men? So far from such a blasphemous thought, that they affirm the direct contrary, and compare all their inspired teachings and instructions to the dead works of bare planting and watering, and which must continue dead, till life comes into them from another and much higher power. " I have planted," says St. Paul, " Apollos has watered, but God gave the increase." And then further to show that this planting and watering, which was the highest work that an inspired apostle could do, was yet in itself to be considered as a lifeless, powerless thing, he adds, " So then, neither is he that planteth anything, nor he that watereth, but God that giveth the increase." But now, if this must be said of all that which the inspired apostles taught in outward words, that it was nothing in itself, was without power, without life, and only such a preparation towards life, as is that of planting and watering, must not that same be said of their inspired teachings when left behind them in writing? For what else are the apostolical scriptures, but those very instructions and teachings put into writing, which they affirmed to be but bare planting and watering, quite powerless in themselves, till the living Spirit of God worked with them? Or will anyone say, that what Paul, Peter, John, etc., spoke by inspiration from their own mouths,

was indeed bare planting and watering, in order to
be capable of receiving life from God; but when
these apostolical teachings and instructions were
written on paper, they were raised out of their first
inability, got the nature of God Himself, became
Spirit and life, and might be called the great
quickening power of God, or, as the Doctor says, the
constant abode and supreme illumination of His
Spirit with us.

It would be great folly and perverseness to charge
me here with slighting or lessening the true value,
use, and importance of the inspired apostolical scriptures; for if the charge was just, it must lie against
Paul, and not against me, since I say nothing of them,
but that which he says, and in his own express
words, namely, that all their labour of preaching,
instructing, and writing by divine inspiration, had
in themselves no other nature, use, or power than
that of such planting and watering as could not
fructify till a higher power than was in them
gave life and growth to that which they planted and
watered.

I exceedingly love and highly reverence the divine
authority of the sacred writings of the apostles and
evangelists, and would gladly persuade everyone to
be as deeply affected with them, and pay as profound
a regard to them, as they would to an Elijah, a St.
John Baptist, or a Paul, whom they knew to be
immediately sent from heaven with God's message to
them. I reverence them as a literal truth of and
from God, as much the greatest heavenly blessing that
can be outwardly bestowed upon us. I reverence
them as doing, or fitted to do all that good amongst

Christians now, which the apostles did in their day, and as of the same use and benefit to the Church of every age, as their planting and watering was to the first.

But now, if this is not thought that fulness of regard that is due to the holy messengers of God; if anyone will still be so learnedly wise as to affirm, that though Paul's preaching in his epistles, whilst he was alive, was indeed only bare planting and watering, but the same epistles, being published after his death, got another nature, became full of divine and living power, such a one has no right to laugh (as the Doctor does) at the silly Mohammedan, who believes the Alcoran to be uncreated. For wherever there is divine efficacy, there, there must be an uncreated power. And if, as the Doctor says, the Scriptures of the New Testament are the only constant abode and supreme illumination of the Spirit of God with us, all that is said of the eternal Spirit of God, of the uncreated light, might and ought to be said of them; that they are the Word that was God, was with God, and are our true Immanuel, or God within us.

27. All Knowledge to be Sacrificed to the Glory of the Gospel.

I shall now only add this friendly hint to the Doctor, that he has a remedy at hand in his own sermon, how he may be delivered from thus grossly mistaking the Spirit of the gospel, as well as the Law of Moses. St. Paul (says the Doctor) " had a quick and lively imagination, and an extensive and intimate acquaintance with those masters in moral painting, the classic writers (N.B.), all which he proudly sacrificed to the glory of the everlasting gospel."[1]

Now if the Doctor did that, though it was only from humility, which he says the apostle did proudly, such humility might be as great a good to him as that pride was to the apostle. And, indeed, one would have thought, that as soon as the Doctor had discovered these writers to be only great masters in moral painting, it should have had the same effect upon him, as if he had found them great masters in delusion. For where there is moral painting, there, there is moral delusion. And the spirit, the life, the purity, and divine simplicity of gospel truth is more eluded, lost, and destroyed by moral paintings, whether in books or pulpits, than by any material colourings put upon images of wood or clay to excite spiritual devotion in churches. Again, if the everlasting gospel is now as glorious a thing, as it was in St. Paul's days; if the highest, most accomplished classic knowledge is so unsuitable to the light and spirit of the gospel, that it is fit for nothing but to be cast away, or as the Doctor says, "to be all sacrificed to the glory of the gospel," how wonderful is it, that this should never come into his head from the beginning to the end of his three long *Legation* volumes, or that he should come piping hot with fresh and fresh classic beauties found out by himself in a Shakespeare, a Pope, etc., to preach from the pulpit the divine wisdom of a Paul, in renouncing all his great classic attainments as mere loss and dung, that by so doing he might win Christ, and be found in Him!

Let it be supposed, that our Lord was to come again

[1] *Sermons*, vol. i. p. 229.

for a while in the flesh, and that His coming was for
this end, to do that for the Christian world cumbered
with much learning, which He did to poor Martha,
only cumbered with much serving, who thereby
neglected that good part which Mary had chosen;
must we suppose that the Doctor would hasten to
meet Him with his sacred alliances, his bundles of
pagan trash, and hieroglyphic profundities, as his full
proof that Mary's good part, which shall never be
taken from her, had been chosen for himself and all
his readers? As well might it be thought, that the
pope would come richly laden with his blessed images,
his heavenly decrees, his divine bulls, as infallible
proofs of his being born again from above, and solely
devoted to the one thing needful.

Let the Doctor figure to himself the gaudy pageantry
of a divine high mass in a Romish cathedral; let him
wonder at that flagrant daring contrariety that it hath
to that first Gospel-Church of Christ, namely, "where
two or three are gathered together in My name, there
am I in the midst of them"; would he not be still fuller
of wonder, if he should hear the pope declaring, that
all this heathenish show of invented fopperies was his
projected defence of that first Church of Christ?
But if the Doctor would see a Protestant wonder full
as great, he need only look at his own theatrical
parading show of heathen mysteries, and heathenish
learning, set forth in highest pomp. To what end?
Why, to bring forth, what he calls (as the pope above)
his projected defence of Christianity.

O vainest of all vain projects! For what is Christianity, but that which Christ was while on earth?
What can it be, but that which it is, and has from

Him? He is a King, who has all power in heaven and on earth, and His kingdom, like Himself, is not of this world. Away then with the projects of popish pomp, and pagan literature to support it; they are as wise contrivances, as a high tower of Babel to defend it against the gates of hell.

28. Something more than Sound Understanding needed to receive the Teaching of the Spirit.

I come now to the quotation from the pastoral letter of Mr. Stinstra. "A judicious writer" (says the *Dissertation*) "observes, that sound understanding and reason are that on which, and by which, God principally operates (N.B.) when He finds it proper to assist (N.B.) our weakness by His Spirit."[1]

I cannot more illustrate the sense, or extol the judgment, both of the author, and quoter of this striking passage, than by the following words:—

"A judicious naturalist observes, that sound and strong lungs are that on which, and by which, the air or spirit of this world principally operates, when (N.B.) he finds it proper to assist, (N.B.) the weakness of our lungs, by his breathing into them." Now, if any right-minded man should happen to find his heart edified, his understanding enlightened, by the above passage on divine inspiration, he will be much pleased at my assuring him, that the pastoral letter of Mr. Stinstra, and the dissertation on enthusiasm by Mr. Green, are from the beginning to the end full as good, in every respect, as that is.

[1] *Dissertation*, p. 73.

These two instances are proof enough, that as soon as any man trusts to natural abilities, skill in languages, and commonplace learning, as the true means of entering into the kingdom of God, a kingdom, which is nothing else but righteousness, peace, and joy in the Holy Ghost, he gives himself up to certain delusion, and can escape no error that is popular, or that suits his state and situation in the learned, religious world. He has sold his birthright in the gospel state of divine illumination, to make a figure and noise with the sounding brass and tinkling cymbals of the natural man.

Whence is it, that we see genius and natural abilities to be equally pleased with, and equally contending for the errors and absurdities of every system of religion, under which they are educated? It is because genius and natural abilities are just the same things, and must have the same nature now, as they had in the ancient schools of the peripatetic, academic, stoic, and atheistical philosophers. "The temptation of honour, which the academic exercise of wit" (as Dr. W. says) "was supposed to bring to its professor,"[1] has still its power among Church disputants. Nor can it possibly ever be otherwise, till parts and genius, etc., do, as the blind, the deaf, the dumb, and lepers formerly did, go to be healed of their natural disorders by the inspiration of that oracle, who said, "I am the light of the world, he that followeth Me, walketh not in darkness." "No man cometh unto the Father but by Me." Well therefore might St. Paul say, "I have determined to know nothing among you, but Christ, and Him crucified." And had it not been

[1] *Divine Legation of Moses*, bk. i. p. 33.

for this determination, he had never known, what he then knew, when he said, " the life that I now live, is not mine, but Christ's that liveth in me." Now, did the apostle here overstretch the matter? Was it a spirit of enthusiasm, and not of Christ living in him, that made this declaration? Was he here making way for ignorance and darkness to extinguish the light that came down from heaven, and was the light of the world? Did he here undermine the true ground and rock on which the Church of Christ was to stand, and prevail against the gates of hell? Did he by setting up this knowledge, as the best and only knowledge that an apostle need to have, break down the fences of Christ's vineyard, rob the Church of all its strongholds, leave it defenceless, without a pale, and a ready prey to infidels? Who can say this, but that " spirit of antichrist, that confesseth not that Jesus Christ is come in the flesh?" For, as Christ's intending nothing, knowing nothing, willing nothing, but purely and solely the whole course of His crucifying process, was the whole truth of His being come in the flesh, was His doing the whole will of Him that sent Him, was His overcoming the world, death, and hell, so he that embraces this process, as Christ embraces it, who is wholly given up to it, as Christ was, he has the will of Christ, and the mind of Christ, and therefore may well desire to know nothing else. To this man alone, is the world, death, and hell, known to be overcome in him, as they were in Christ; to him alone is Christ become the resurrection and the life; and he that knows this, he knows with St. Paul that all other knowledge may and will be cast away as dung. Now, if St. Paul, having rejected all other knowledge but that of a crucified Saviour, which to the Jew was a stumblingblock, and to the Greek foolishness, if he had afterwards wrote three such *Legation* volumes as the Doctor has done, for the food and nourishment of Christ's sheep, who can have no life in them but by eating the true bread that came down from heaven, must they not have been called Paul's full recantation of all that he had taught of a Christ crucified ?

29. All Knowledge of the Spirit dependent upon His dwelling in us.

The other instance of delusion from book-learning, relates to Mr. Green, who, wanting to write on divine inspiration, runs from book to book, from country to country, to pick up reports wherever he could find them, concerning divine inspiration, from this and that judicious author, that so he might be sure of compiling a judicious dissertation on the subject. All which he might have known to be mere delusion and lost labour, had he but remembered, or regarded any one single saying either of Christ or His apostles concerning the Holy Spirit and His operations. For not a word is said by them, but fully shows that all know ledge or perception of the Spirit is nothing else but the enjoyment of the Spirit, and that no man can know more of Him than that which the Spirit Himself is, and does, and manifests of His power in man.

"The things of God," says St. Paul, "knoweth no man, but the Spirit of God." Is not this decisive upon the matter ? Is not this proof enough, that nothing in man but the Spirit of God in him, can know what the Spirit's work in man is and does ?

The fruits of the Spirit, so often mentioned in Scripture, are not things different, or separate from the Spirit; and if the Spirit is not always working in us, His fruits must be as absent from us as He is. St. John says, "Hereby we know that He abideth in us, by the Spirit which He hath given us." A demonstration, that the Spirit can no other way make Himself known to us, but by His dwelling and working in us. St. James says, "Every good and perfect gift cometh from above": but now does not he in reality deny this, who seeks for the highest gift of knowledge from below, from the poor contrivance of a commonplace book? Again, "If any man lacketh wisdom, let him ask it of God"; St. James does not say, let him go ask Peter, or Paul, or John, because he knew that divine wisdom was nothing else, but divine inspiration. But Mr. Green has got together his ingenious, his eminent writers, his excellent, learned, judicious authors, his cool, rational-morality doctors (a set of men whose glorious names we read no more of in the gospel, than of the profound Aristotle, or the divine Cicero), and these are to do that for him, which the whole College of Apostles could do for nobody.

Now this doctrine, that nothing but the Spirit can know the things that be of God, and that the enjoyment of the Spirit, is all the knowledge we can have of Him, is a truth taught us, not only by all Scripture, but by the whole nature of things. For everything that can be seen, known, heard, felt, etc., must be manifested by itself, and not by another. It is not possible for anything but light to manifest light, nor for anything but darkness to make darkness to be

known. Yet this is more possible, than for anything
but divine inspiration to make divine inspiration to be
known. Hence there is a degree of delusion still
higher, to be noted in such writers as Mr. Green; for
his collection of ingenious, eminent, rational authors,
of whom he asks counsel concerning the necessity or
certainty of the immediate inspiration of the Spirit,
are such as deny it, and write against it. Therefore
the proceeding is just as wise, as if a man was to
consult some ingenious and eminent atheists, about
the truth and certainty of God's immediate continual
providence; or ask a few select deists, how, or what
he was to believe of the nature and power of gospel
faith. Now, there are the Holy Spirit's own operations, and there are reports about them. The only
true reports, are those that are made by inspired
persons; and if there were no such persons, there
could be no true reports of the matter. And therefore
to consult uninspired persons, and such as deny and
reproach the pretence to inspiration, to be rightly
instructed about the truth of immediate continual
divine inspiration, is a degree of blindness greater
than can be charged upon the old Jewish scribes and
Pharisees.

30. Only the Holy Spirit can give the Real Possession of what Scripture relates.

The reports that are to be acknowledged as true
concerning the Holy Spirit and His operations, are
those that are recorded in Scripture; that is, the
Scriptures are an infallible history, or relation of that
which the Holy Spirit is, and does, and works in true

believers ; and also an infallible direction how we are
to seek, and wait, and trust in His good power over us.
But then the Scriptures themselves, though thus true
and infallible in these reports and instructions about the
Holy Spirit, yet they can go no further than to be a
true history ; they cannot give to the reader of them
the possession, the sensibility, and enjoyment of that
which they relate.   This is plain, not only from the
nature of a written history or instruction, but from
the express words of our Lord, saying, " Except a man
be born again of the Spirit, he cannot see or enter into
the kingdom of God."   Therefore the new birth from
above, or of the Spirit, is that alone which gives true
knowledge and perception of that which is the kingdom of God.   The history may relate truths enough
about it ; but the kingdom of God, being **nothing else
but the power and presence of God, dwelling and
ruling in our souls,** this can only manifest itself, and
can manifest itself to nothing in man but to the new
birth.   For everything else in man is deaf and dumb
and blind to the kingdom of God ; but when that which
died in Adam is made alive again by the quickening
Spirit from above, this being the birth which came at
first from God, and a partaker of the divine nature,
this knows, finds, and enjoys the kingdom of God.

" I am the way, the truth, and the life," says
Christ : this record of Scripture is true ; but what a
delusion for a man to think that he knows and finds
this to be true, and that Christ is all this benefit and
blessing to him, because he assents, consents, and
contends, it may be, for the truth of those words.
This is impossible.   The new birth is here again the
only power of entrance ; everything else knocks at the

door in vain: I know you not, says Christ, to everything, but the new birth. " I am the way, the truth,
and the life; " this tells us neither more nor less,
than if Christ had said, I am the kingdom of God, into
which nothing can enter, but that which is born of the
Spirit.

Here again may be seen, in the highest degree of
certainty, the absolute necessity of immediate divine
inspiration through every part of the Christian life.
For if a birth of the Spirit is that alone that can
enter into, or receive the kingdom of God come
amongst men, that alone which can find Christ to be
the way, the truth, and the life, then a continual life
or breathing of the Spirit in us, must be as necessary
as the first birth of the Spirit. For a birth of the
Spirit is only to make a beginning of a life of the
Spirit: birth is only in order to life; if therefore the
life of the Spirit continues not, the birth is lost, and
the cessation of its breathing in us is nothing else but
death again to the kingdom of God, that is, to everything that is or can be godly. Therefore the
immediate continual inspiration of the Spirit, as the
only possible power and preservation of a godly life,
stands upon the same ground, and is as absolutely
necessary to salvation as the new birth.

31. The Difference between a mere Letter-
learned Knowledge and that which the
Divine Life within us gives.

Take away this power and working life of the
Spirit from being the one life of all that is done in
the Church, and then, though it be ever so outwardly

glorious in its extent, or ever so full of learned
members, it can be nothing else in the sight of God
but the wise Greeks and the carnal Jews become a
body of water-baptized Christians. For no one can
be in a better state than this ; the wisdom of the Greek,
the carnality of the Jew, must have the whole government of him, till he is born of and led by the Spirit of
God ; this alone is the kingdom of God, and everything else is the kingdom of this world, in which
Satan is declared to be the prince. Poor, miserable
man ! that strives, with all the sophistry of human
wit, to be delivered from the immediate continual
operation and government of the Spirit of God, not
considering that where God is not, there is the devil,
and where the Spirit rules not, there all is the work
of the flesh, though nothing be talked of but spiritual
and Christian matters. I say talked of ; for the best
ability of the natural man can go no further than talk,
and notions, and opinions about Scripture words and
facts ; in these he may be a great critic, an acute
logician, a powerful orator, and know everything of
Scripture, except the Spirit and the truth.

How much then is it to be lamented, as well as
impossible to be denied, that though all Scripture
assures us, that the things of the Spirit of God are
and must, to the end of the world, be foolishness to
the natural man, yet from one end of learned Christendom to the other, nothing is thought of as the true and
proper means of attaining a divine knowledge, but
that which every natural, selfish, proud, envious, false,
vain-glorious, worldly man can do. Where is that
divinity student who thinks, or was ever taught to
think, of partaking of the light of the gospel in any

other way, than by doing with the Scriptures that which he does with pagan writers, whether poets, orators, or comedians, namely, exercise his logic, rhetoric, and critical skill, in descanting upon them ? This done, he is thought by himself, and often by others, to have a sufficiency of divine apostolical knowledge. What wonder, therefore, if it should sometimes happen, that the very same vain, corrupt, puffing literature, that raises one man to be a poet-laureate, should set another in a divinity chair.

How is it that the logical, critical, learned deist comes by his infidelity ? Why, just by the same help of the same good powers of the natural man, as many a learned Christian comes to know, embrace, and contend for the faith of the gospel. For, drop the power and reality of divine inspiration, and then all is dropped that can set the believer above, or give him any godly difference from the infidel. For the Christian's faith has no goodness in it, but that it comes from above, is born of the Spirit ; and the deist's infidelity has no badness in it, but because it comes from below, is born of the will of flesh and of the will of men, and rejects the necessity of being born again out of the corruption of fallen nature. The Christian therefore that rejects, reproaches, and writes against the necessity of immediate divine inspiration, pleads the whole cause of infidelity : he confirms the ground on which it stands ; and has nothing to prove the goodness of his own Christianity, but that which equally proves to the deist the goodness of his infidelity. For without the new birth, or which is the same thing, without immediate continual divine inspiration, the difference between the Christian and the infidel is quite lost; and whether the uninspired unregenerate son of Adam be in the Church, or out of the Church, he is still that child of this world, that fallen Adam, and mere natural man, to whom the things of the Spirit of God are and must be foolishness. For a full proof of this no more need be seen, than that which you cannot help seeing, that the same shining virtues, and the same glaring vices are common to them both. For the Christian not made such by the Spirit of God continually inspiring and working in him, has only a Christianity of his own making, and can have only such appearances of virtues, and will have such reality of vices, as natural self wants to have. Let him therefore renounce what is called natural religion as much as he will, yet unless he is a new-born and divinely-inspired Christian, he must live and die in all his natural corruption.

Through all Scripture nothing else is aimed at or intended for man, as his Christianity, but the divine life, nor anything hinted at, as having the least power to raise or beget it, but the holy life-giving Spirit of God. How gross therefore is that blindness, which reading the gospel, and the history of gospel Christians, cannot see these two fundamental truths: (1) "That nothing is divine knowledge in man, but the divine life;" (2) "That the divine life is nothing else but a birth of the divine nature within him"?

But this truth being lost or given up, vain learning and a worldly spirit, being in possession of the gospel-book, set up kingdoms of strife and division. For what end? Why, that the unity of the Church may not be lost. Multiply systems of empty notions and opinions. For what? Why, that words and forms may do that for the Church now, which to the first Church, of Christ's own forming, could only be done by being born of the Spirit.

Hence it is, that the Scripture scholar is looked upon as having divine knowledge of its matters, when he is as ready at chapter and verse, as the critic is at every page of Cicero. And nothing is looked upon as defective in divinity knowledge, but such supposed mistakes of the genius of the Hebrew, or Greek letter, as the sublime students of immortal words of a Milton, or a Shakespeare, charge as blunders upon one another.

Now to call such Scripture skill divine knowledge, is just as solid and judicious, as if a man was said, or thought to know, that which St. John knew, because he could say his whole Gospel and Epistles by heart, without missing a word of them. For a literal knowledge of Scripture is but like having all Scripture in the memory, and is so far from being a divine perception of the things spoken of, that the most vicious, wicked scholar in the world may attain to the highest perfection in it. But divine knowledge and wickedness of life are so inconsistent, that they are mutual death and destruction to one another ; where the one is alive, the other must be dead. Judas Iscariot knew Jesus Christ, and all that he said and did to His crucifixion ; he knew what it was to be at the Lord's Table, and to partake of His supper of bread and wine. But yet, with much more truth it may be said, that he knew nothing of all this, and had no better a knowledge of it than Pontius Pilate had. Now all knowledge of Christ, but that which is from divine inspiration, or the new birth, is but as poor and profitless, as Judas his knowledge was. It may say to Christ, as he did,

Hail, Master; but no one can call Jesus Lord, but by
the Holy Spirit. This empty letter-learned knowledge,
which the natural man can as easily have of the sacred
Scripture and religious matters as of any other books
or human affairs, this being taken for divine knowledge, has spread such darkness and delusion all over
Christendom, as may be reckoned no less than a
general apostasy from the gospel state of divine
illumination. For the gospel state is in its whole
nature nothing else; it has but one light, and that is
the Lamb of God; it has but one life, and that is by
the Spirit of God. Whatever is not of and from this
light, and governed by this Spirit, call it by what high
name you will, is no more a part of the gospel state,
nor will have a better end, than that which entereth
into the mouth, and corrupteth in the belly.

32. The Kingdom of God is only where the Light and Spirit of God dwell and rule.

That one Light and Spirit, which was only one from
all eternity, before angels or any heavenly beings
were created, must to all eternity be that one only
Light and Spirit, by which angels or men can ever
have any union or communion with God. Every
other light is but the light whence beasts have their
sense and subtlety; every other spirit is but that
which gives to flesh and blood all its lusts and appetites. Nothing else but the loss of the one Light and
Spirit of God turned an order of angels into devils.
Nothing else but the loss of that same Light and Spirit
took from the divine Adam his first crown of paradisaical glory, stripped him more naked than the

beasts, and left him a prey to devils, and in the jaws of eternal death. What therefore can have the least share of power towards man's redemption but the Light and Spirit of God making again a birth of themselves in Him, as they did in His first glorious creation? Or what can possibly begin, or bring forth this return of his first lost birth, but solely that which is done by this eternal Light and Spirit. Hence it is, that the gospel state is by our Lord affirmed to be a kingdom of heaven at hand, or come among men, because it has the nature of no worldly thing or creaturely power, is to serve no worldly ends, can be helped by no worldly power, receives nothing from man but man's full denial of himself, stands upon nothing that is finite or transitory, has no existence but in that working power of God that created and upholds heaven and earth, and is a kingdom of God become man, and a kingdom of men united to God, through a continual immediate divine illumination. What scripture of the New Testament can you read that does not prove this to be the gospel state, a kingdom of God, into which none can enter but by being born of the Spirit, none can continue to be alive in it but by being led by the Spirit, and in which not a thought, or desire, or action can be allowed to have any part in it, but as it is a fruit of the Spirit?

" Thy kingdom come, Thy will be done on earth as it is in heaven." What is God's kingdom in heaven, but the manifestation of what God is, and what He does in His heavenly creatures? How is His will done there, but because His Holy Spirit is the life, the power, and mover of all that live in it. We

daily read this prayer, we extol it under the name of
the Lord's Prayer, and yet (for the sake of orthodoxy)
preach and write against all that is prayed for in it.
For nothing but a continual, essential, immediate
divine illumination can do that which we pray may
be done.

For where can God's kingdom be come, but where
every other power but His is at an end, and driven
out of it ?   How can His will only be done, but where
the spirit that wills in God wills in the creature ?

33. Trust in the Wisdom of Men the cause of the Fall of the Church from its first state.

What now have parts, and literature, and the
natural abilities of man that they can do here ?
Just as much as they can do at the resurrection
of the dead ; for all that is to be done here is nothing
else but resurrection and life.   Therefore, that which
gave eyes to the blind, cleansed the lepers, cast out
devils, and raised the dead, that alone can and must
do all that is to be done in this gospel kingdom of
God.   For every the smallest work or fruit of grace
must be as solely done by God as the greatest miracle
in nature ; and the reason is, because every work of
grace is the same overcoming of nature, as when the
dead are raised to life.   Yet vain man would be
thought to be something, to have great power and
ability in this kingdom of grace, not because he
happens to be born of noble parents, is clothed in
purple and fine linen, and fares sumptuously every
day, but because he has happened to be made a

scholar, has run through all languages and histories, has been long exercised in conjectures and criticisms, and has his head as full of all notions, theological, poetical, and philosophical, as a dictionary is full of all sorts of words.

Now let this simple question decide the whole matter here: Has this great scholar any more power of saying to this mountain, " Be thou removed hence, and cast into the sea," than the illiterate Christian has ? If not, he is just as weak, as powerless, and little in the kingdom of God as he is. But if the illiterate man's faith should happen to be nearer to the bulk of a grain of mustard-seed than that of the prodigious scholar, the illiterate Christian stands much above him in the kingdom of God.

Look now at the present state of Christendom, glorying in the light of Greek and Roman learning (which an age or two ago broke forth) as a light that has helped the gospel to shine with a lustre that it scarce ever had before. Look at this, and you will see the fall of the present Church from its first gospel state to have much likeness to the fall of the first divine man from the glory of paradisaical innocence and heavenly purity into an earthly state, and bestial life of worldly craft and serpentine subtlety.

In the first Gospel-Church heathen light had no other name than heathen darkness; and the wisdom of words was no more sought after than that friendship of the world which is enmity with God. In that new-born Church, the tree of life, which grew in the midst of Paradise, took root and grew up again. In the present Church, the tree of life is hissed at, as the visionary food of deluded enthusiasts; and the tree of

death, called the tree of knowledge of good and evil,
has the eyes and hearts of priest and people, and is
thought to do as much good to Christians as it did
evil to the first inhabitants of Paradise.   This tree,
that brought death and corruption into human nature
at first, is now called a tree of light, and is day and
night well watered with every corrupt stream, however distant, or muddy with earth, that can be drawn
to it.

The simplicity, indeed, both of the gospel letter and
doctrine, has the shine and polish of classic literature
laid thick upon it.   Cicero is in the pulpit, Aristotle
writes Christian ethics, Euclid demonstrates infidelity
and absurdity to be the same thing.   Greece had but
one Longinus, Rome had but one Quintilian; but in
our present Church they are as common as patriots in
the State.

But now, what follows from this new-risen light?
Why, Aristotle's atheism, Cicero's height of pride and
depth of dissimulation, and every refined or gross
species of Greek and Roman vices, are as glaring in
this new enlightened Christian Church as ever they
were in old pagan Greece or Rome.   Would you find
a gospel-Christian in all this midday glory of learning,
you may light a candle, as the philosopher did in the
midday sun, to find an honest man.

34. Of Self. The Denial of our own Wisdom the chief part of Self-denial.

And indeed, if we consider the nature of our salvation, either with respect to that which alone can save
us, or that from which we are to be saved, it will be

plain, that the wit and elegance of classic literature, brought into a Christian Church to make the doctrines of the Cross have a better salvation effect upon fallen man, is but like calling in the assistance of balls and masquerades to make the lent-penitence go deeper into the heart, and more effectually drive all levity and impurity out of it. How poorly was the gospel at first preached, if the wisdom of words and the gifts of natural wit and imagination had been its genuine helps? But alas, they stand in the same contrariety to one another as self-denial and self-gratification. To know the truth of gospel salvation is to know that man's natural wisdom is to be equally sacrificed with his natural folly; for they are but one and the same thing, only called sometimes by one name, and sometimes by the other.

His intellectual faculties are, by the fall, in a much worse state than his natural animal appetites, and want a much greater self-denial. And when own will, own understanding, and own imagination have their natural strength indulged and gratified, and are made seemingly rich and honourable with the treasures acquired from a study of the belles-lettres, they will just as much help poor fallen man to be likeminded with Christ, as the art of cookery, well and daily studied, will help a professor of the gospel to the spirit and practice of Christian abstinence. To know all this to be strictly the truth, no more need be known than these two things: (1) That our salvation consists wholly in being saved from ourselves, or that which we are by nature; (2) That in the whole nature of things nothing could be this salvation or saviour to us but such an humility of God manifested

in human nature, as is beyond all expression. Hence
the first unalterable term of this Saviour to fallen man
is this, " Except a man denies himself, forsakes all that
he has, yea and his own life, he cannot be My disciple."
And to show that this is but the beginning, or ground
of man's salvation, the Saviour adds, " Learn of Me,
for I am meek and lowly of heart." What a light is
here for those that can bear or love the light! Self
is the whole evil of fallen nature; self-denial is our
capacity of being saved; humility is our saviour.
This is every man's short lesson of life, and he that
has well learnt it, is scholar enough, and has had all
the benefit of a most finished education. Then old
Adam with all his ignorance is cast out of him; and,
when Christ's humility is learnt, then he has the very
mind of Christ, and that which brings him forth a son
of God.

Who then can enough wonder at that bulk of
libraries, which has taken place of this short lesson of
the gospel, or at that number of champion disputants,
who, from age to age, have been all in arms to
support and defend a set of opinions, doctrines, and
practices, all which may be most cordially embraced,
without the least degree of self-denial, and most firmly
held fast, without getting the least degree of humility
by it?

What a grossness of ignorance, both of man and his
Saviour, to run to Greek and Roman schools to learn
how to put off Adam and to put on Christ? To drink
at the fountain of pagan poets and orators, in order
more divinely to drink of the cup that Christ drank
of? What can come of all this, but that which is
already too much come, a Ciceronian-gospeller, in stead

of a gospel-penitent? Instead of the depth, the truth and spirit of the humble publican, seeking to regain Paradise, only by a broken heart, crying, " God, be merciful to me, a sinner," the high-bred classic will live in daily transports at the enormous [1] sublime of a Milton, flying thither on the unfeathered wings of high-sounding words.

This will be more or less the case with all the salvation doctrines of Christ, whilst under classical acquisition and administration. Those divine truths, which are no further good and redeeming, but as they are spirit and life in us, which can have no entrance, or birth, but in the death of self, in a broken and contrite heart, will serve only to help classic painters (as Dr. W.[2] calls them) to lavish out their colours on their own paper monuments of lifeless virtues.

How came the learned heathens by their pride and vanity, by their inability to come under the humility of the Cross? It was because the natural man shined in the false glory of his own cultivated abilities. Have wit and parts, an elegant taste, any more good or redeeming virtue in Christians, than they had in heathens? As well might it be said that own will is good, and has a redeeming virtue in a Christian, but bad and destructive in a heathen. I said a redeeming virtue in it; because nothing is or can be a religious good to fallen man, but that which has a redeeming

---

[1] See Milton's *Enormous Bliss.*

[2] As this Address was wrote some time ago, in which are certain strictures upon Dr. Warburton's writings, who has lately been consecrated a Right Reverend Lord Bishop, I thought it more candid not to alter my style, than to take the advantage of charging such gross errors on a Bishop of Gloucester, which I only found in a Mr. and Dr. Warburton.

virtue in it, or is, so far as it goes, a true renewal of
the divine life in the soul. Therefore, said our only
Redeemer, "Without Me, ye can do nothing." Whatever is not His immediate work in us is at best but a
mere nothing with respect to the good of our redemption. A Tower of Babel may to its builders' eyes seem
to hide its head in the clouds, but as to its reaching
of heaven, it is no nearer to that than the earth on
which it stands. It is thus with all the buildings of
man's wisdom and natural abilities in the things of
salvation; he may take the logic of Aristotle, add to
that the rhetoric of Tully, and then ascend as high as
he can on the ladder of poetic imagination, yet no
more is done to the reviving the lost life of God in
his soul than by a tower of brick and mortar to reach
heaven.

Self is the root, the tree, and the branches of all
the evils of our fallen state. We are without God,
because we are in the life of self. Self-love, self-
esteem, and self-seeking are the very essence and life
of pride; and the devil the first father of pride, is
never absent from them, nor without power in them.
To die to these essential properties of self is to
make the devil depart from us. But as soon as we
would have self-abilities have a share in our good
works, the satanic spirit of pride is in union with us,
and we are working for the maintenance of self-love,
self-esteem, and self-seeking.

All the vices of fallen angels and men have their
birth and power in the pride of self, or I may better
say, in the atheism and idolatry of self; for self is
both atheist and idolater. It is atheist, because it
has rejected God; it is an idolater, because it is its

own idol. On the other hand, all the virtues of the heavenly life are the virtues of humility. Not a joy, or glory, or praise in heaven, but is what it is through humility. It is humility alone that makes the unpassable gulf between heaven and hell. No angels in heaven, but because humility is in all their breath; no devils in hell, but because the fire of pride is their whole fire of life.

35. Of Pride and Humility, and the reason why the need of Self-denial is so absolute.

What is then, or in what lies the great struggle for eternal life? It all lies in the strife between pride and humility: all other things, be they what they will, are but as under workmen; pride and humility are the two master powers, the two kingdoms in strife for the eternal possession of man.

And here it is to be observed that every son of Adam is in the service of pride and self, be he doing what he will, till a humility that comes solely from heaven has been his redeemer. Till then, all that he doth will be only done by the right hand, that the left hand may know it. And he that thinks it possible for the natural man to get a better humility than this from his own right reason (as it is often miscalled) refined by education, shows himself quite ignorant of this one most plain and capital truth of the gospel, namely, that there never was, nor ever will be, but one humility in the whole world, and that is the one humility of Christ, which never any man, since the fall of Adam, had the least degree of but from Christ. Humility is one, in the same sense and truth, as Christ is one, the Mediator is one, redemption is one. There are not two Lambs of God that take away the sins of the world. But if there was any humility besides that of Christ, there would be something else besides Him that could take away the sins of the world. "All that came before Me," says Christ, "were thieves and robbers": we are used to confine this to persons; but the same is as true of every virtue, whether it has the name of humility, charity, piety, or anything else; if it comes before Christ, however good it may pretend to be, it is but a cheat, a thief, and a robber under the name of a godly virtue. And the reason is, because **pride and self have the all of man, till man has his all from Christ.** He therefore only fights the good fight, whose strife is, that the self-idolatrous nature which he hath from Adam may be brought to death, by the supernatural humility of Christ brought to life in him.

The enemies to man's rising out of the fall of Adam, through the Spirit and power of Christ, are many. But the one great dragon enemy, called antichrist, is **self-exaltation.** This is his birth, his pomp, his power, and his throne; when self-exaltation ceases, the last enemy is destroyed, and all that came from the pride and death of Adam is swallowed up in victory.

There has been much sharp looking-out to see where and what antichrist is, or by what marks he may be known. Some say he has been in the Christian world almost ever since the gospel times, nay, that he was even then beginning to appear and show himself. Others say he came in with this or that pope; others that he is not yet come, but near at hand. Others will have it that he has been here, and there, but driven from one place to another by several new risen Protestant sects.

But to know with certainty where and what antichrist is, and who is with him, and who against him, you need only read this short description which Christ gives of Himself. "(1) I can do nothing of Myself. (2) I came not to do My own will. (3) I seek not My own glory. (4) I am meek and lowly of heart." Now if this is Christ, then self-ability or self-exaltation, being the highest and fullest contrariety to all this, must be alone the one great antichrist, that opposes and withstands the whole nature and Spirit of Christ.

What therefore has everyone so much to fear, to renounce and abhor, as every inward sensibility of self-exaltation, and every outward work that proceeds from it. But now, at what things shall a man look, to see that working of self which raises pride to its strongest life, and most of all hinders the birth of the humble Jesus in his soul? Shall he call the pomps and vanities of the world the highest works of self-adoration? Shall he look at fops and beaux, and painted ladies, to see the pride that has the most of antichrist in it? No, by no means. These are indeed marks, shameful enough, of the vain, foolish heart of man, but yet, comparatively speaking, they are but the skin-deep follies of that pride which the fall of man has begotten and brought forth in him. Would you see the deepest root, and iron-strength of pride and self-adoration, you must enter into the dark chamber of man's fiery soul, where the light of God (which alone gives humility and meek submission to

all created spirits) being extinguished by the death
which Adam died, Satan, or which is the same thing,
self-exaltation became the strong man that kept possession of the house, till a stronger than he should
come upon him.   In this secret source of an eternal
fiery soul, glorying in the astral light of this world,
a swelling kingdom of pomps and vanities is set up in
the heart of man, of which, all outward pomps and
vanities are but its childish transitory playthings. The
inward strong man of pride, the diabolical self, has his
higher works within; he dwells in the strength of the
heart, and has every power and faculty of the soul
offering continual incense to him. His memory, his
will, his understanding, his imagination, are always at
work for him, and for no one else. His memory is
the faithful repository of all the fine things that self
has ever done; and lest anything of them should be
lost or forgotten, she is continually setting them before
his eyes. His will, though it has all the world before it,
yet goes after nothing, but as self sends it. His understanding is ever upon the stretch for new projects to
enlarge the dominions of self; and if this fails, imagination comes in, as the last and truest support of self,
she makes him a king and mighty lord of castles in
the air.

This is that full-born natural self, that must be
pulled out of the heart, and totally denied, or there
can be no disciple of Christ; which is only saying this
plain truth, that the apostate self-idolatrous nature of
the old man must be put off, or there can be no new
creature in Christ

36. Natural Reason and the Glory of Learning the great Stronghold of Self and Pride.

Now what is it in the human soul that most of all hinders the death of this old man? What is it that above all other things strengthens and exalts the life of self, and makes it the master and governor of all the powers of the heart and soul? It is the fancied riches of parts, the glitter of genius, the flights of imagination, the glory of learning, and the self-conceited strength of natural reason; these are the strongholds of fallen nature, the master-builders of pride's temple in the heart of man, and which, as so many priests, keep up the daily worship of idol-self. And here let it be well, and well observed, that all these magnified talents of the natural man are started up through his miserable fall from the life of God in his soul. Wit, genius, learning, and natural reason would never have had any more a name among men, than blindness, ignorance, and sickness, had man continued, as at first, an holy image of Father, Son, and Holy Spirit. Everything then that dwelt in him, or came from him, would have only said so much of God, and nothing of himself, have manifested nothing to him but the heavenly powers of the triune life of God dwelling in him. He would have had no more sense or consciousness of his own wit, or natural reason, or any power of goodness in all that he was, and did, than of his own creating power, at beholding the created heavens and earth. It is his dreadful fall from the life of God in his soul, that has furnished him with these high intellectual riches, just as it has furnished him with the substantial riches of his bestial appetites and lusts. And when the lusts of the flesh have spent out their life, when the dark thick body of earthly flesh and blood shall be forced to let the soul go loose, all these bright talents will end with that system of fleshly lusts, in which they begun; and that of man which remains will have nothing of its own, nothing that can say, I do this, or I do that; but all that it has or does, will be either the glory of God manifested in it, or the power of hell in full possession of it. The time of man's playing with parts, wit, and abilities, and of fancying himself to be something great and considerable in the intellectual world, may be much shorter, but can be no longer, than he can eat and drink with the animals of this world. When the time comes, that fine buildings, rich settlements, acquired honours, and Rabbi, Rabbi, must take their leave of him, all the stately structures, which genius, learning, and flights of imagination, have painted inwardly on his brain and outwardly on paper, must bear full witness to Solomon's vanity of vanities.

Let then the high accomplished scholar reflect, that he comes by his wit, and parts, and acute abilities just as the serpent came by his subtlety; let him reflect, that he might as well dream of acquiring angelic purity to his animal nature by multiplying new invented delights for his early passions and tempers, as of raising his soul into divine knowledge through the well-exercised powers of his natural reason and imagination.

The finest intellectual power, and that which has the best help in it towards bringing man again into the region of divine light, is that poor despised thing called simplicity. This is that which stops the workings of the fallen life of nature, and leaves room for God to work again in the soul according to the good pleasure of His holy will. It stands in such a waiting posture before God, and in such readiness for the divine birth, as the plants of the earth wait for the inflowing riches of the light and air. But the self-assuming workings of man's natural powers shut him up in himself, closely barred up against the inflowing riches of the Light and Spirit of God.

Yet so it is, in this fallen state of the Gospel-Church, that with these proud endowments of fallen nature, the classic scholar, full fraught with pagan light and skill, comes forth to play the critic and orator with the simplicity of salvation mysteries; mysteries which mean nothing else but the inward work of the triune God in the soul of man, nor any other work there, but the raising up a dead Adam into a living Christ of God.

However, to make way for parts, criticism, and language-learning, to have the full management of salvation doctrines, the well-read scholar gives out that the ancient way of knowing the things of God, taught and practised by fishermen apostles, is obsolete. They indeed wanted to have divine knowledge from the immediate continual operation of the Holy Spirit, but this state was only for a time, till genius and learning entered into the pale of the Church. Behold, if ever, " the abomination of desolation standing in the holy place ! " For as soon as the doctrine is set up, that man's natural parts and acquired learning have full right and power to sit in the divinity chair, and to guide men into that truth which was once the

only office and power of the Holy Spirit, as soon as
this is done, and so far as it is received, it may with
the greatest truth be said that the kingdom of God
is entirely shut up, and only a kingdom of scribes,
Pharisees, and hypocrites can come instead of it.
For by this doctrine the whole nature and power of
gospel religion is much more denied than by setting
up the infallibility of the pope; for though his claim
to infallibility is false, yet he claims it from and under
the Holy Spirit; but the Protestant scholar has his
divinity knowledge, his power in the kingdom of
truth, from himself, his own logic and learned reason.
Christ has nowhere instituted an infallible pope; and
it is full as certain that He has nowhere spoke one
single word, or given the least power to logic, learning,
or the natural powers of man in His kingdom.   He
has never said to them, "Whatsoever ye shall bind on
earth shall be bound in Heaven"; never said to them,
"Go ye and teach all nations," no more than He has
ever said to wolves, "Go ye and feed my sheep."
Christ indeed said of Himself, according to the flesh,
"It is expedient for you that I go away."   But where
has He said of Himself, according to the Spirit, "It is
also expedient for you that I go away, that your own
natural abilities and learned reason may have the
guidance of you into all truth"?   This is nowhere said,
unless logic can prove it from these words, "Without
Me you can do nothing," and "Lo, I am with you to
the end of the world."

37. The true nature of the Kingdom of Heaven.

The first and main doctrine of Christ and His apostles was to tell the Jews " that the kingdom of God was at hand," or was come to them. Proof enough surely that their Church was not that kingdom of God, though by God's appointment, and under laws of His own commanding. But why not, when it was thus set up by God? It was because it had human and worldly things in it, consisted of carnal ordinances, and had only types, and figures, and shadows of a kingdom of God that was to come. Of this kingdom Christ says, " My kingdom is not of this world"; and as a proof of it, He adds, " If it was of this world, then would My servants fight for Me"; which was saying, that it was so different in kind, and so superior in nature to this world, that no sort of worldly power could either help or hinder it. But of this world, into which the kingdom of God was come, the Holy One of God says, " In the world ye shall have tribulation; but be of good comfort, I have overcome the world." Now how was it that Christ's victory was their victory? It was because He was in them and they in Him, " Because I live, ye shall live also; in that day ye shall know that I am in the Father, and you in Me, and I in you."

This was the kingdom of God come to them, the same kingdom of God in which Adam was born and begun his first glorious life, when the image and likeness of the Holy Trinity had an outward glory, like that which broke through the body of Christ, when on Mount Tabor " His face did shine as the sun, and

His raiment was as white as the light." To the children of this kingdom, says its Almighty King, " When they bring you before magistrates and powers, take no thought how or what ye shall answer, or what ye shall say unto them, for the Holy Ghost shall teach you in that same hour what ye ought to say. For it is not ye that speak, but the Spirit of your Father that speaketh in you."

No higher or other thing is here said than in these other words, " Take no thought what ye shall eat or drink, or wherewithal ye shall be clothed, but seek first the kingdom of God, and His righteousness, and all these things shall be added unto you." This is the truth of the kingdom of God come unto men, and this is the birthright privilege of all that are living members of it, to be delivered from their own natural spirit which they had from Adam, from the spirit and wisdom of this world, and through the whole course of their lives only to say, and do, and be that which the Spirit of their Father worketh in them.

But now is not this kingdom gone away from us, are we not left comfortless, if instead of this Spirit of our Father speaking, doing, and working everything in us and for us, we are left again to our own natural powers, to run to every Lo here and Lo there to find a share in that kingdom of God, which once was, and never can be anything else but God, the wisdom and power of God manifested in our flesh ? Had it not been as well, nay better for us, to have been still under types and figures, sacrificing bulls and goats by divine appointment, than to be brought under a religion that must be spirit and life, and then left to the jarring interests of the wisdom of the Greek and

the carnality of the Jew how to be living members of
it ?   For where the Spirit of God is not the continual
immediate governor of spiritual things, nothing better
can come of it.   For the truth and full proof of this,
no more need be appealed to than all the libraries
and churches of Christendom for many ages to this
day.

38. Man needs to be Saved from his own Wisdom as much as from his own Righteousness.

What is the difference between man's own righteousness and man's own light in religion ?   They are
strictly the same thing, do one and the same work,
namely, keep up and strengthen every evil, vanity,
and corruption of fallen nature.   Nothing saves a
man from his own righteousness but that which saves
and delivers him from his own light.   The Jew that
was most of all set against the gospel, and unable to
receive it, was he that trusted in his own righteousness; this was the rich man, to whom it was as hard
to enter into the kingdom of heaven as for a camel
to go through the eye of a needle.   But the Christian
that trusts in his own light is the very Jew that trusted
in his own righteousness; and all that he gets by the
gospel is only that which the Pharisee got by the law,
namely, to be further from entering into the kingdom
of God than publicans and harlots.   How comes it
that a beast, a scarlet whore, a horned dragon, and
other the most horrible descriptions of diabolical
power, have been by the Spirit of God made descriptions of the Christian Church ?   How comes it that

the Spirit describes the Gospel-Church as driven into
a wilderness;—the two faithful witnesses, Moses and
Jesus, as prophesying so many ages in sackcloth, and
slain in the streets of spiritual Sodom and Egypt?
It is because man's own natural light, man's own
conceited righteousness, his serpentine subtlety, his
self-love, his sensual spirit and worldly power, have
seized the mysteries of salvation that came down from
heaven, and built them up into a kingdom of envious
strife and contention, for learned glory, spiritual
merchandise, and worldly power. This is the beast,
the whore, and dragon, that has governed, and will
govern in every private Christian, and public Church,
till, dead to all that is self, they turn to God;
not to a God that they have only heard of with
their ears, and their fathers have told them, but
to a God of life, light, and power, found living and
working within them, as the essential life, light, and
power of their own lives. For God is only our God,
by a birth of His own divine nature within us. This,
and nothing but this, is our whole relation to, our
only fellowship with Him, our whole knowledge of
Him, our whole power of having part in the mysteries
of gospel-salvation. Nothing can seek the kingdom
of God, or hunger and thirst after His righteousness,
nothing can cry " Abba Father," nothing can pray, " Thy
kingdom come," nothing can say of Christ, " My Lord
and my God," but that which is born of God, and is
the divine nature itself become creaturely in us.
Nothing but God in man can be a godly life in man.

39. The Letter killeth, but the Spirit giveth Life.

Hence is that of the apostle, " The letter killeth, but the Spirit giveth life." But you will say, Can this be true of the spiritual divine letter of the gospel ? Can it kill, or give death ? Yes, it kills, when it is rested in ; when it is taken for divine power, and supposed to have goodness in itself ; for then it kills the Spirit of God in man, quenches His holy fire within us, and is set up instead of it. It gives death when it is built into systems of strife and contention about words, notions, and opinions, and makes the kingdom of God to consist, not in power, but in words. When it is thus used, then of necessity it kills, because it keeps from that which alone is life and can give life. This then is the whole of the matter ; all the literal truths, and variety of doctrines and expressions of the written word, have but one nature, one end, and one errand, they all say nothing else to man but that one thing which Christ said, in these words, " Come unto Me, all ye that labour and are heavy laden, and I will refresh you " ; just the same, as when it is said, " Jesus Christ, who is of God made unto us wisdom, righteousness, and sanctification " ; this is the only refreshment from Christ. Again, " But ye are washed, but ye are cleansed in the name of our Lord Jesus " ; just the same as when it is said, " Except ye abide in Me, and I in you, ye have no life in you." Again, " By grace ye are saved, by faith ye are saved," says neither more nor less than this, " He that eateth My flesh, and drinketh My blood, hath eternal life " ; the same as when Christ

says, " Without Me ye can do nothing "; the same as
the apostle says, " Yet not I, but Christ that liveth
in me "; the same as " Christ in us the hope of glory;
if Christ be not in you, ye are reprobates." Therefore
to come to Christ, to have our heavy-laden, fallen
nature refreshed by Him, to be born spirit of His
Spirit, to have His heavenly flesh and heavenly blood
made living in us, before we put off the bestial body
and blood of death which we have from Adam, is the
one only thing taught and meant by all that is so
variously said in the Scriptures of the merits and
benefits of Christ to us. It is the spirit, the body,
the blood of Christ within us that is our whole peace
with God, our whole adoption, our whole redemption,
our whole justification, our whole glorification; and
this is the one thing said and meant by that new
birth of which Christ says, " Except a man be born
again from above, he cannot enter into the kingdom
of God." Now, the true ground why all that is said
of Christ in such a variety of expressions has only one
meaning, and points only to one and the same thing,
is this, it is because the whole state and nature of
fallen man wants only one thing, and that one thing is
a real birth of the divine nature made living again in
him, as at the first; and then all is done, that can
be done, by all the mysteries of the birth, and whole
process of Christ, for our salvation. All the Law, the
Prophets, and the Gospel are fulfilled, when there is in
Christ a new creature, having life in and from Him,
as really as the branch has its life in and from the
vine. And when all Scripture is thus understood,
and all that either Christ says of Himself, or His
apostles say of Him, are all heard, or read, only as

one and the same call to come to Christ, in hunger
and thirst to be filled and blessed with His divine
nature made living within us; then, and then only,
the letter kills not, but as a sure guide leads directly
to life. But grammar, logic, and criticism, knowing
nothing of Scripture but its words, bring forth nothing
but their own wisdom of words, and a religion of
wrangle, hatred, and contention, about the meaning of
them.

But lamentable as this is, the letter of Scripture
has been so long the usurped province of school
critics, and learned reasoners making their markets
of it, that the difference between literal, notional, and
living divine knowledge, is almost quite lost in the
Christian world. So that if any awakened souls are
here or there found among Christians, who think that
more must be known of God, of Christ, and the
powers of the world to come, than every scholar can
know by reading the letter of Scripture, immediately
the cry of enthusiasm, whether they be priests or
people, is sent after them. A procedure, which could
only have some excuse, if these critics could first
prove, that the apostle's text ought to be thus read,
The Spirit killeth, but the letter giveth life.

40. The distinction between Literal and Divine Knowledge almost lost in the Christian Church.

The true nature, and full distinction between literal
and divine knowledge, is set forth in the highest
degree of clearness in these words of our Saviour,
" The kingdom of God is like a treasure in a field ":

thus far is the true use and benefit, and utmost power of the letter, it can tell us of a treasure that we want, a treasure that belongs to us, and how and where it is to be found; but when it is added, that a "Man goes and sells all that he has, and buys that field," then begins the divine knowledge, which is nothing else but the treasure possessed and enjoyed. Now, what is here said is the same that is said in these other words of Christ, "Except a man denies himself and forsakes all that he hath, he cannot be My disciple"; that is, he cannot partake of My mind, My spirit, and My nature, and therefore cannot know Me; he is only a hearer of a treasure, without entering into the possession and enjoyment of it. And thus it is with all Scripture, the letter can only direct to the doing of that which it cannot do, and give notice of something that it cannot give.

Now, clear and evident as this distinction is, between a mere literal direction to a thing, and a real participation of it, which alone is a true perception of it, the generality of Christians seem quite insensible of any other religious perception or knowledge of divine things, but such ideas or notions of them as a man can form from Scripture words. Whereas good and evil, the only objects of religious knowledge, are an inward state and growth of our life, they are in us, are a part of us, just in the same manner as seeing and hearing are in us, and we can have no real knowledge of them any other way, than as we have of our own seeing and hearing. And as no man can get or lose his seeing or hearing, or have less or more of them, by any ideas or notions that he forms about them, just so it is with that which is the power of good, and the power of evil in us; notions and ideas have no effect upon it. Yet no other knowledge is thought of, or sought after, or esteemed of any value, but that which is notional and the work of the brain.

Thus, as soon as a man of speculation can demonstrate that which he calls the being and attributes of God, he thinks, and others think, that he truly knows God. But what excuse can be made for such an imagination, when plain Scripture has told him that to know God is eternal life? that is, to know God is to have the power, the life, and the Spirit of God manifested in him, and therefore it is eternal life. "No man knoweth the Father, but the Son, and he to whom the Son revealeth Him." Because the revelation of the Son is the birth of the Son in the soul, and this new creature in Christ has alone knowledge of God, what He is, and does, and works in the creature.

Again, another, forming an opinion of faith from the letter of Scripture, straightway imagines that he knows what faith is, and that he is in the faith. Sad delusion! For to know what faith is, or that we are in the faith, is to know that Christ is in us of a truth; it is to know the power of His life, His sufferings, His death, His resurrection and ascension, made good in our souls. To be in the faith, is to have done with all notions and opinions about it, because it is found and felt by its living power and fruits within us, which are righteousness, peace, and joy in the Holy Ghost. All which are three names of powers peculiar to Jesus Christ; He alone is our righteousness, our peace, our joy in the Holy Ghost. And therefore faith is not in us, by reason of this or that opinion, assent or consent, but it is Christ, or the divine nature in us; or its operations could not be righteousness, peace, and joy in the Holy Ghost. By faith ye are saved, has no other meaning than by Christ ye are saved. And if faith in its whole nature, in its root and growth, was anything else but Christ, or a birth of the divine nature within us, it could do us no good, no power could be ascribed to it, it could not be our victory, it could not overcome the world, the flesh, and the devil. Every faith that is not Christ in us is but a dead faith.

How trifling, therefore (to say no worse of it), is that learning which sets up a difference between faith and its works, between a justification by faith, and justification by its works. Is there any difference between Christ as a Redeemer and His redeeming works? Can they be set above one another in their redeeming efficacy? If not, then faith and its works, which are nothing else but Christ in us, can have no separation from, or excellency above one another, but are strictly one, as Christ is one, and no more two things than our Saviour and our salvation are two different things in us. Everything that is said of faith, from Adam to this day, is only so much said of the power, and life of a one redeeming Christ, working within us; so that to divide faith from its works is as absurd as to divide a thing from its self, a circle from its roundness. No salvation would have ever been ascribed to faith, but because it is, in the strictest sense, Christ Himself, the power of God, living and working in us. It never would have been said of faith, that every power of the world, the flesh, and the devil, must yield to it, but because it is that very Christ within us, without whom we can do nothing. But if without Christ we can do nothing, and yet all things are possible to our faith, can there be a fuller demonstration that our faith is nothing else but Christ born, and living within us? Whatever, therefore, there is of power within us that tends to salvation, call it by what name you will, either faith, or hope, or prayer, or hunger after the kingdom of God and His righteousness, it is all but one power, and that one is Christ within us. If, therefore, faith and its good works are but one and the same Christ living in us, the distinction between a good faith and its good works, and all the contentious volumes that have been written about it, are as mere ignorant jargon, as a distinction made and contended for, between life and its living operations.

When the holy Church of Christ, the kingdom of God came among men, was first set up, it was the apostle's boast, that all other wisdom or learning was sunk into nothing. "Where," says he, "is the wise, the scribe, the disputer of this world? Hath not God made them foolishness?" But now, it is the boast of all churches, that they are full of the wise, the scribes, the disputers of this world, who sit with learned pomp in the apostle's chair, and have the mysteries of the kingdom of God committed to them.

Hence it is, that from a religion of heavenly love, built upon the redeeming life and doctrines of a Son of God dying to save the whole world, division, bitterness, envy, pride, strife, hatred, and persecution, nay every outrage of war and bloodshed, breathe and break forth with more strength in learned Christendom than

ever they did from a religion of pagan idolatry, set up
by Satan.

41. Love the only Key to true Knowledge.

It may perhaps be here said, must there then be no
learning or scholarship, no recondite erudition in the
Christian Church? Must there be nothing thought
of, or got by the gospel, but mere salvation? Must
its ministers know nothing, teach nothing, but such
salvation-doctrines as Christ and His apostles taught;
nothing but the full denial of self, poverty of spirit,
meekness, and humility, and unwearied patience, a
never-ceasing love, an absolute renunciation of the
pomps and vanities of the world, a full dependence
upon our heavenly Father; no joy or rejoicing but in
the Holy Ghost; no wisdom but that which God
gives; no walking but as Christ walked; no reward
or glory for their labours of love, but that of being
found in Christ, flesh of His flesh, bone of His bones,
spirit of His Spirit, and clothed with the wedding-
garment when the bridegroom comes, "when the Lord
Himself shall descend from heaven with a shout, with
the voice of the archangel, and with the trumpet of
God, and the dead in Christ shall rise first"?

To this the first answer is, Happy, thrice happy are
they, who are only the thus learned preachers of the
gospel, who through all their ministry, seek nothing
for themselves or others, but to be taught of God;
hunger after nothing but the bread of life that came
down from heaven, owning no master but Christ, no
teacher but His Holy Spirit; as unable to join with
the diggers in pagan pits of learning, as with those

that "labour for the wind, and give their money for
that which is not bread."

Secondly, with regard to the demand of learned
knowledge in the Christian Church, it may be
answered, that all that has been said above, is only
for the increase and promotion of it, and that all
ignorance and darkness may be driven quite out of it.
The Church of Christ is the seat or school of all the
highest knowledge that the human nature is capable
of in this life.   Ignorance is everywhere but in the
Church of Christ.   The Law, the Prophets, and the
Gospel, are the only treasures of all that can be called
the knowledge either of God or man ; and He in whom
the Law, the Prophets, and the Gospel are fulfilled,
is the only well-educated man, and one of the first-
rate scholars in the world.   But now, who is he, that
has this wisdom from these rich treasures ?   Who is
he, in whom all is known and fulfilled which they
teach ?   The lip of truth has told us, that it is he,
and he alone, " who loves God with all his heart, with
all his soul, with all his mind, and with all his
strength, and his neighbour as himself."   This is the
man that is all wisdom, all light, and let into full
possession of all that is meant by all the mysteries
contained in the Law, the Prophets, and the Gospel.
Where this divine love is wanting, and a diabolical
self sits in its place, there may be great wits, shining
critics, orators, poets, etc., as easily as there may be a
profound Machiavel, a learned Hobbs, or an atheistical
virtuoso.   But would you divinely know the mysteries
of nature, the ground and reason of good and evil in
this world, the relation and connection between the
visible and invisible world, how the things of time

proceed from, are influenced by, and depend upon the things and powers of eternity, there is but one only key of entrance; nothing can open the vision, but seeing with the eyes of that same love, which begun and carries on all that is, and works in visible and invisible nature. Would you divinely know the mysteries of grace and salvation, would you go forth as a faithful witness of gospel truths, stay till this fire of divine love has had its perfect work within you. For till your heart is an altar, on which this heavenly fire never goes out, you are dead in yourself, and can only be a speaker of dead words, about things that never had any life within you. For without a real birth of this divine love in the essence of your soul, be as learned and polite as you will, your heart is but the dark heart of fallen Adam, and your knowledge of the kingdom of God will be only like that which murdering Cain had. For everything is murder, but that which love does. If love is not the breath of your life, the spirit that forms and governs everything that proceeds from you, everything that has your labour, your allowance and consent, you are broken off from the works of God, you have left His creation, you are without God, and your name, and nature, and works, can have no other name, or nature, but that which is called pride, wrath, envy, hypocrisy, hatred, revenge, and self-exaltation, under the power of Satan in his kingdom of darkness. Nothing can possibly save you from being the certain prey of all these evil spirits, through the whole course of your life, but a birth of that love which is God Himself, His light, and Spirit within you.

There is no knowledge in heaven, but what proceeds

from this birth of love, nor is there any difference between the highest light of an angel, and the horrid darkness of a devil, but that which love has made. But now, since divine love can have no beginning, but from a birth of the divine nature in us, therefore says St. John, we love Him because He **first** loved us, the same as saying, we desire God, because He first desired us; for we could not desire God, but because He first desired us, we could not turn to God, but because He first turned to us. And so it is, that we could not love God, but because He first loved us, that is, because He first by our creation brought forth, and by our redemption continued and kept up that same birth of His own Spirit of Love in us. For as His Holy Spirit must first be a gift to us, or born in us, and then we have that which can worship God in spirit, so **His love must of all necessity be a gift to us**, or born in us, and then we have that of God in us which alone can love Him with His own love. A truth absolutely asserted in these words : " Love is of God, and he that loveth, is born of God."

Let this be my excuse to the learned world, for owning no school of wisdom, but where the one only lesson is divine love; and the one only teacher the Spirit of God. Let no one call this wild or extravagant; it is no wilder a step, no more injurious to man, to truth and goodness, than the owning no God but one. For to be called from everything but divine love and the Spirit of God, is only being called from everything that has the curse of fallen nature in it. And no man can come from under this curse, till he is born again of divine love, and the Spirit of God. For thus to be born, is as much the one sole happiness, joy, and glory of men, both now and ever, as it is the sole joy and glory of angels eternally in the heavens. Believe me then, thou great scholar, that all that thou hast got of wisdom or learning, day after day, in any other school but this, will stand thee in as much stead, fill thee with as high heavenly comfort at the hour of death, as all the long dreams, which night after night, thou hast ever had in thy sleep. And till a man knows this, with as much fulness of conviction as he knows the vanity of a dream, he has his full proof, that he is not yet in the light of truth, not yet taught of God, nor likeminded with Christ.

One of Christ's followers said, "Lord, suffer me first to go and bury my father"; the answer was, "Let the dead bury their dead; follow thou Me." Another said to Him, "Let me first go bid them farewell, that are at home in my house"; Jesus answered, "No man having put his hand to the plough, and looking back, is fit for the kingdom of God." Now let it be supposed that a third had said, "Lord, I have left several deep-learned books at home, written by the greatest masters of grammar, logic, and eloquence, suffer me first to go back for them, lest losing the light which I had from them, I might mistake the depth and truth of Thy heavenly doctrines, or be less able to prove and preach them powerfully to others." Would not such a request as this have had a folly and absurdity in it, not chargeable upon those two other requests which Christ rejected? And yet, what can scholastic, classic, and critical divinity say for itself, but that very same thing, which this requester here said?

42. Human Wisdom, without the Light of God born in the Soul, is but the Darkness of Nature.

The Holy Jesus said, "I am the light of the world, he that followeth Me, walketh not in darkness." Here spiritual light and darkness are as immutably fixed, and separated from one another, as the light and darkness of this world were divided on the first day of the creation.   Jesus Christ, the eternal Son of God, is the one only light both of men and angels.   Fallen nature, the selfish will, proud tempers, the highest abilities, the natural sagacity, cunning arts and subtleties, that are or can be in fallen men and angels, are nothing else but their fulness of spiritual darkness, from which nothing but works of darkness can come forth.   In a word, darkness is the whole natural man ; light is the new-born man from above.   Therefore says the Christ of God, "I am the light of the world," because He alone is the birth of heaven in the fallen souls of men. But now, who can more reject this divine light, or more plainly choose darkness instead of it, than he who seeks to have his mind enriched, the faculties of his fallen soul cultivated by the literature of poets, orators, philosophers, sophists, sceptics, and critics, born and bred up in the worship and praises of idol gods and goddesses ?   What is this, but like going to the serpent to be taught the innocent spirit of the dove ; or to the elegant lusts of Anacreon and Ovid, to learn purity of heart, and kindle the flame of heavenly love in our souls ?   Look where you will, this is the wisdom of those who seek to pagans for skill to work in Christ's vineyard ; who from long

labours in restoring the grammar, and finding out the
hidden beauties of some old vicious book, set up for
qualified artists to polish the gospel pearl of great
price. Surely this is no better a proof of their savour-
ing the things that are of God, than Peter gave, when
his Master said to him, " Get thee behind Me, Satan."
A grave ecclesiastic, bringing forth out of his closet
skilful meditations on the commentaries of a murdering Cæsar, or the sublime rhapsody of an old Homer,
or the astonishing beauties of a modern Dunciad, has
as much reason to think that he is walking in the
light of Christ, and led by the Spirit of God, as they
have who are only eating and drinking, and rising up
to play.

43. We need the Fire and Spirit of Heaven.

But to see the exceeding folly of expecting ability
in divine knowledge, from anything that is the wit,
wisdom, or spirit of the natural man, you need only
read these words of the holy messenger of God, the
Elias that was to come. " I indeed," says he, " baptize
you with water, but He that cometh after me, whose
shoe's latchet I am not worthy to unloose, He shall
baptize you with the Holy Ghost, and with fire."
Now if this which the Baptist said of Christ is not
our faith, if we do not receive it as the truth in which
we are firmly to stand, then, be as learned as we will,
we have no better a faith, or higher wisdom, than
those blind rabbies who received not the testimony of
John. A fire and Spirit from above was the news
which he published to the world; this, and nothing

else, was his kingdom of God that was at hand. Now if this fire and Spirit from above has not baptized us into a birth of the life of God in our souls, we have not found that Christ and kingdom of God, to which John bore witness. But if (what is still worse) we are so bewitched through the sorcery of learning, as to turn writers and preachers against this inward, and only redeeming heavenly fire and Spirit, we are baptized with the spirit of those to whom our Lord said, "Woe unto you scribes, Pharisees, hypocrites, for ye shut up the kingdom of heaven against men; for ye neither go in yourselves, neither suffer ye them that are entering to go in."

For what is, or can be the fall of a divine Adam under the power of sin, Satan, and hell, but the extinction of that heavenly fire and Spirit, which was his first union with God and all heavenly beings. Say now, that he had not this heavenly fire and Spirit at the first, that nothing lived or breathed in him but that astral fire and spirit which is the life and spirit of all earthly animals, and then you have a religion as divine as that of the old Sadducees, who allowed of no resurrection, angel, or Spirit. For, deny the truth and fulness of a divine life in the first man, and then his fall and redemption are equally empty sounds about nothing. For what can he be fallen from, or redeemed to, if he has now all that fire and spirit of life which he ever had, or ought to have, and if all that is more than this, is but the fiction and dream of a distempered brain? Tell me, why that burning and shining light, that man that was more than a prophet, should come with his water, and the Son of God, God of God, should come with his fire-baptism, if man neither wanted,

nor could receive a higher water, and fire of light,
than that which he has in common with the beasts of
the field ?   Why is there all this stir about religions,
expiations, and atonements, why all these priestly
ordinations, consecrations, churches, sacraments, and
prayers ?   For if the fire and spirit of this world is
the one life, and highest life, both of man and beasts,
we have it unasked for, and on the same terms as the
beasts have it, and can only lose it, as they do when
they lose their existence.

But if fire and Spirit from heaven can alone make
heavenly creatures, and us, to be children of an
heavenly Father; if the Son of God took our fallen
nature upon Him, that the first heavenly fire and
Spirit might again come to life in us, if divine life,
divine light, and divine goodness, can only come from
them, and only in such degree, as they are kindled in
our souls, what a poverty of sense is it in those who
are called to a resurrection of the first divine life,
where a new creature is taught by that same unction
from above whence all the angels and principalities
of heaven have their light and glory, what a poverty
of sense, I say, in such, to set themselves down at the
feet of a master Tully and a master Aristotle, who
only differ from the meanest of all other corrupt men,
as the teaching serpent differed from his fellow-animals,
by being more subtle than all the beasts of the
field.

Behold then your state, ye ministers, that wait at
Christian altars, who will have neither faith, nor hope,
nor desire of heavenly fire kindled in your souls, you
have a priesthood, and an altar not fit to be named
with that, which in Jewish days had a holy fire from

God descending upon it which made priest and sacrifice acceptable to God, though only type and pledge of that inward celestial fire, which Christ would kindle into a never-ceasing burning, in the living temples of His new-born children from above.

Complain then no more of atheists, infidels, and suchlike open enemies to the gospel kingdom of God; for whilst you call heavenly fire and Spirit, kindled into the same essential life in us as they are in holy angels, downright frenzy, and mystic madness, you do all that infidel work within the Church, which they do on the outside of it. And if through a learned fear of having that done to your earthly reason, which was done to Enoch when God took him, you will own no higher a regeneration, no more birth of God in your souls, than can be had by a few cold drops of water sprinkled on the face, any of the heathen gods of wood and stone are good enough for such an elementary priesthood. For let this be told you, as a truth from God, that till heavenly fire and Spirit have a fulness of a birth within you, you can rise no higher by your highest learning, than to be elegant orators about Scripture words.

44. The Kingdom of God is within you.

Our Lord has said, " The kingdom of God is within you," that is, the heavenly fire and Spirit, which are the true kingdom and manifestation of God, are within you. And indeed, where can it be else? Yet what learned pains are taken to remove the literal meaning from these words, as too visionary a thing for learned ears. And yet it is a truth obvious to common sense, that even this outward world of stars and elements, neither does, nor can belong to us, or we to it, but so far as it is, literally speaking, a kingdom within us. For the outward kingdom or powers of this world signify nothing to a worldly man that is dead; but no man is dead, but because the kingdom of this world, with all its powers of fire, light, and spirit, stands only outwardly about him, but has lost its life and power within him.

Say now, out of reverence to sound literature, and abhorrence of enthusiasm, that the kingdom of God is not really and virtually within, that its heavenly fire, light, and Spirit, are not, ought not to be born in a sober right-minded follower of Christ, and then you have a good disciple of Christ, as absolutely dead to the kingdom of heaven, as the corpse that has nothing of the fire, spirit, and light of this world in it, is dead to all the outward world round about it.

What a sobriety of faith and sound doctrine is it, to preach up a necessity of being living members of the kingdom of heaven, and at the same time the necessity of orthodoxly holding, that a heavenly birth neither is, nor can, nor ought to be within us! For if it either is, or could, or ought to be within us, then it could not be a brain-sick folly to believe, that the literal words of Christ had no deceit, falsity, or delusion in them, when he said, " Except a man be born again from above, he cannot see, or enter into the kingdom of God." That is, he cannot possibly have any godlike or divine goodness, he cannot be a child of an heavenly Father, but from the nature and Spirit of his heavenly Father brought to a real birth of life in Him. Now if, without this divine birth, all that we have in us is but fallen Adam, a birth of sin, the flesh, and the devil, if the power of this heavenly birth is all the power of goodness that is or was, or ever can be in a son of Adam; and if logic, learning, and criticism, are almost everywhere set in high places, to pronounce and prove it to be mere enthusiasm and spiritual frenzy, what wonder is it, if folly of doctrine, wickedness of life, lusts of the flesh, profaneness of spirit, wantonness of wit, contempt of goodness, and profession of Christianity should all of them seem to have their full establishment among us?

What wonder, if sacraments, church prayers, and preachings, leave high and low, learned and unlearned, men and women, priests and people, as unaltered in all their aged vices, as they leave children unchanged in their childish follies? For where the one only fountain of life and goodness is forsaken, where the seed of the divine birth is not alive, and going forwards in the birth, all the difference between man and man is as nothing with respect to the kingdom of God. It matters not what name is given to the old earthly man of Adam's bestial flesh and blood, whether he be called a zealous Churchman, a stiff-necked Jew, a polite civilised heathen, or a grave infidel; under all these names, the unregenerate old man has but one and the same nature, without any other difference, but that which time, and place, education, complexion, hypocrisy, and worldly wisdom, happen to make in him. By such a one, whether he be Papist, or Protestant, the gospel is only kept as a book, and all that is within it is only so much condemnation to the keeper, just as the old man, a Jew, has kept the Book

of the Law and Prophets, only to be more fully condemned by them.

45. The Christian, not owning the Holy Spirit as the fulfilling of the Gospel, is in the same fallen state as the Jew not owning Christ as the fulfilling of the Law.

That the Jewish and Christian Church stand at
this day in the same kind of apostasy, or fallen state,
must be manifest to everyone, that will not shut his
eyes against it. Why are the Jews in a fallen state ?
It is because they have refused Him, who in His
whole process was the truth, the substance, the life,
and fulfilling of all that which was outwardly taught,
and prescribed in their Law and Prophets.

But is it not as easy to see that the whole Christian
Church are in a fallen state, and for the same reason,
because they are fallen or turned away from that
Holy Spirit who was promised, and given to be the one
only power, life, and fulfilling of all that which was
outwardly taught, and prescribed by the gospel. For
the Holy Spirit to come was just the same all, and
fulfilling of the whole gospel, as a Christ to come was
the all, and the fulfilling of the Law. The Jew
therefore with his Old Testament, not owning Christ
in all his process to be the truth and life, and fulfiller
of their Law, is just in that same apostasy, as the
Christian with his New Testament, not owning the
Holy Spirit in all his operations, to be his only light,
guide, and governor. For as all types and figures in
the Law were but empty shadows without Christ's

being the life and power of them, so all that is written in the gospel is but dead letter, unless the Holy Spirit in man be the living reader, the living rememberer, and the living doer of them. Therefore, where the Holy Spirit is not thus owned and received, as the whole power and life of the gospel state, it is no marvel that Christians have no more of gospel virtues than the Jews have of patriarchal holiness, or that the same lusts and vices which prosper amongst Jews, should break forth with as much strength in fallen Christendom. For the New Testament not ending in the coming of the Holy Spirit, with fulness of power over sin and hell, and the devil, is but the same, and no better a help to heaven, than the Old Testament without the coming of a Messiah. Need I now say any more, to demonstrate the truth of that which I first said was the one thing absolutely essential, and only available to man's salvation, namely, the Spirit of God brought again to His first power of life in us. This was the glory of man's creation, and this alone can be the glory of His redemption. All besides this, that passes for a time betwixt God and man, be it what it will, shows only our fall and distance from God, and in its best state has only the nature of a good road, which is only good, because that which we want is at the end of it. Whilst God calls us by various outward dispensations, by creaturely things, figurative institutions, etc., it is a full proof, that we are not yet in our true state, or that union with God which is intended by our redemption.

God said to Moses, " Put off thy shoes, for the place whereon thou standest is holy ground." Now this which God said to Moses, is only that very same

thing, which circumcision, the Law, sacrifices, and
sacraments, say to man. They are in themselves
nothing else but outward significations of inward
impurity, and lost holiness, and can do no more in
themselves, but intimate, point, and direct to an
inward life and new birth from above, that is to be
sought after.

46. Of Mistaking the Outward for the Inward.

But here lies the great mistake, or rather idolatrous
abuse of all God's outward dispensations. They are
taken for the thing itself, for the truth and essence of
religion. That which the learned Jews did with the
outward letter of their Law, that same do learned
Christians with the outward letter of their gospel.
Why did the Jewish Church so furiously and obsti-
nately cry out against Christ, "Let Him be crucified"?
It was because their letter-learned ears, their worldly
spirit, and temple-orthodoxy, would not bear to hear
of an inward Saviour, not bear to hear of being born
again of His Spirit, of eating His flesh, and drinking
His blood, of His dwelling in them, and they in Him.
To have their law of ordinances, their temple-pomp
sunk into such a fulfilling Saviour as this, was such
enthusiastic jargon to their ears, as forced their sober,
rational theology, to call Christ, Beelzebub, His doctrine, blasphemy, and all for the sake of Moses and
rabbinic orthodoxy.

Need it now be asked, whether the true Christ of the
gospel be less blasphemed, less crucified, by that
Christian theology which rejects an inward Christ, a

Saviour living and working in the soul, as its inward light and life, generating His own nature and spirit in it, as its only redemption, whether that which rejects all this as mystic madness be not that very same old Jewish wisdom sprung up in Christian theology, which said of Christ when teaching these very things, " He is mad; why hear ye Him ? " Our blessed Lord in a parable sets forth the blind Jews, as saying of Himself, " We will not have this man to reign over us." The sober-minded Christian scholar has none of this Jewish blindness; he only says of Christ, we will not have this man to reign in us, and so keeps clear of such mystic absurdity, as St. Paul fell into, when he enthusiastically said, "Yet not I, but Christ that liveth in me."

Christian doctors reproach the old learned Rabbis, for their vain faith, and carnal desire of a glorious, temporal, outward Christ, who should set up their temple-worship all over tho world. Vanity indeed, and learned blindness enough ?

But nevertheless, in these condemners of rabbinic blindness, St. Paul's words are remarkably verified, namely, " Wherein thou judgest another, thou condemnest thyself, for thou that judgest dost the same thing." For, take away all that from Christ which Christian doctors call enthusiasm, suppose Him not to be an inward birth, a new life and spirit within us, but only an outward, separate, distant heavenly prince, no more really in us, than our high cathedrals are in the third heavens, but only by an invisible hand from His throne on high, some way or other raising and helping great scholars, or great temporal powers, to make a rock in every nation for His Church to stand upon;

suppose all this (which is the very marrow of modern divinity) and then you have that very outward Christ, and that very outward kingdom, which the carnal Jew dreamed of, and for the sake of which the spiritual Christ was then nailed to the Cross, and is still crucified by the new-risen Jew in the Christian Church.

47. The Cause of all Blindness in the Church, as in Paradise, the desire of other Knowledge than comes from God alone.

If it now be asked, whence, or from what, comes all this spiritual blindness, which from age to age thus mistakes and defeats all the gracious designs of God towards fallen mankind? Look at the origin of the first sin, and you see it all. Had Eve desired no knowledge but what came from God, Paradise had been the habitation of her and all her offspring. If after Paradise lost, Jews and Christians had desired no knowledge but what came from God, the Law and Prophets had kept the Jew close to the first tree of life, and the Christian Church had been a kingdom of God, and communion of saints to this day.

But now corruption, sin, death, and every evil of the world, have entered into the Church, the spouse of Christ, just as they entered into Eve, the spouse of Adam in Paradise, in the same way, and from the same cause, namely, a desire of more, or other knowledge, than that which comes from God alone. This desire is the serpent's voice within every man, which does all that to him, and in him, which the serpent at the tree did to Eve. It carries on the first deceit, it shows and recommends to him that same beautiful tree of own will, own wit, and own wisdom, springing up within him, which Eve saw in the garden; and yet so blind is this love of wisdom, as not to see, that his eating of it is in the strictest truth his eating of the same forbidden fruits as Eve did, and keeping up in himself all that death and separation from God, which the first knowledge-hunger brought forth.

Let then the eager searcher into words for wisdom, the book-devourer, the opinion-broker, the exalter of human reason, and every projecting builder of religious systems, be told this, that the thirst and pride of being learnedly wise in the things of God, is keeping up the grossest ignorance of them, and is nothing else but Eve's old serpent, and Eve's evil birth within them, and does no better work in the Church of Christ, than her thirst after wisdom did in the Paradise of God. Speak, Lord, for Thy servant heareth, is the only one way by which any man ever did, or ever can attain divine knowledge, and divine goodness. To knock at any other door but this, is but like asking life of that which is itself dead, or praying to him for bread who has nothing but stones to give.

Now strange as all this may seem to the labour-learned possessor of far-fetched book-riches, yet it is saying no more, nor anything else, but that which Christ said in these words, "Except ye be converted, and become as little children, ye cannot enter into the kingdom of God." For, if classic gospellers, linguist critics, Scripture logicians, salvation orators, able dealers in the grammatic powers of Hebrew, Greek, and Roman phrases, idioms, tropes, figures, etc. etc., can show, that by raising themselves high in these attainments, they are the very men that are sunk

down from themselves into Christ's little children of
the kingdom of God, then it may be also said, that he
who is labouring, scheming, and fighting for all the
riches he can get from both the Indies, is the very
man that has left all to follow Christ, the very man
that "labours not for the meat that perishes."

48. Only he that loveth, knoweth God.

Show me a man whose heart has no desire, or
prayer in it, but to love God with his whole soul and
spirit, and his neighbour as himself, and then you
have shown me the man who knows Christ, and is
known of Him; the best and wisest man in the
world, in whom the first paradisaical wisdom and
goodness are come to life. Not a single precept in
the gospel, but is the precept of his own heart, and
the joy of that new-born heavenly love which is the
life and light of his soul. In this man, all that came
from the old serpent is trod under his feet, not a
spark of self, of pride, of wrath, of envy, of covetousness, or worldly wisdom, can have the least abode in
him, because that love, which fulfilleth the whole Law
and the Prophets, that love which is God and Christ,
both in angels and men, is the love that gives birth,
and life, and growth to everything that is either
thought, or word, or action in him. And if he has no
share or part with foolish errors, cannot be tossed
about with every wind of doctrine, it is because, to be
always governed by this love, is the same thing as to
be always taught of God.

On the other hand, show me a scholar as full of
learning, as the Vatican is of books, and he will be

just as likely to give all that he has for the gospel-pearl, as he would be, if he was as rich as Crœsus. Let no one here imagine, that I am writing against all human literature, arts, and sciences, or that I wish the world to be without them. I am no more an enemy to them, than to the common useful labours of life. It is literal learning, verbal contention, and critical strife about the things of God, that I charge with folly and mischief to religion. And in this, I have all learned Christendom, both Popish and Protestant, on my side. For they both agree in charging each other with a bad and false gospel-state, because of that which their learning, logic, and criticism do for them. Say not then, that it is only the illiterate enthusiast that condemns human learning in the gospel kingdom of God. For when he condemns the blindness and mischief of Popish logic and criticism, he has all the learned Protestant world with him; and when he lays the same charge to Protestant learning, he has a much larger kingdom of Popish great scholars, logically and learnedly affirming the same thing. So that the private person, charging human learning with so much mischief to the Church, is so far from being led by enthusiasm, that he is led by all the church-learning that is in the world.

Again, all learned Christendom agrees in the same charge against temporal power in the Church, as hurtful to the very being and progress of a salvation kingdom that is not of this world, as supporting doctrines that human learning has brought into it. And true it is and must be, that human power can only support and help forward human things. The Protestant brings proof from a thousand years' learn-

ing and doctrines, that the pope is an unjust usurper
of temporal power in the Church, which is Christ's
spiritual spouse. The Papist brings the learning of
so many ages to show that a temporal head of the
Church is an anti-Christian usurpation. And yet
(N.B.) he who holds Christ to be the one, only head,
heart, and life of the Church, and that no man can
call Jesus, Lord, but by the Holy Ghost, passes with
the learned of both these people for a brain-sick
enthusiast.

49. The Departure from the one Mystic Way of Salvation the cause of the Corruption of Christendom.

Is it not then high time to look out for some better
ground to stand upon, than such learning as this ?
Now look where you will, through all the whole nature
of things, no divine wisdom, knowledge, goodness, and
deliverance from sin, are anywhere to be found for
fallen man, but in these two points : (1) a total entire
entrance into the whole process of Christ ; (2) a total
resignation to, and sole dependence upon the continual
operation of the Holy Ghost, or Christ come again in
the spirit, to be our never-ceasing light, teacher, and
guide into all those ways of virtue, in which He
Himself walked in the flesh. All besides this, call it
by what name you will, is but dead work, a vain
labour of the old man to new-create himself. And
here let it be well observed, that in these two points
consists the whole of that mystic divinity, to which a
Jewish orthodoxy at this day is so great an enemy.
For nothing else is meant, or taught by it, but a total

dying to self (called the process or cross of Christ)
that a new creature (called Christ in us, or Christ
come in the spirit), may be begotten in the purity
and perfection of the first man's union with God.
Now, let the Christian world forget, or depart from
this one mystic way of salvation, let anything else be
thought of or trusted to but the cross of Christ, and
the Spirit of Christ, and then, though churches and
preachers and prayers and sacraments are everywhere
in plenty, yet nothing better can come of it than a
Christian kingdom of pagan vices, along with a mouth-
belief of an holy catholic Church, and communion of
saints. To this melancholy truth, all Christendom both
at home and abroad bears full witness. Who need be
told, that there is not a corruption or depravity of
human nature, no kinds of pride, wrath, envy, malice,
and self-love; no sorts of hypocrisy, falseness, cursing,
swearing, perjury, and cheating; no wantonness of
lust in every kind of debauchery, but are as common
all over Christendom as towns and villages.[1]

50. No true Church Reformation but in departing from the Spirit of the World.

In these last ages of fallen Christendom, many
reformations have taken place; but alas! truth must
be forced to say, that they have been in all their
variety, little better than so many runaway births of
one and the same mother, so many lesser Babels come
out of Babylon the great. For among all the re-
formers, the one only true reformation has never yet

[1] Here I omit some pages on serving mammon, oaths, and war as
proof of the state of the Church.

been thought of. A change of place, of governors, of opinions, together with new-formed outward models, is all the reformation that has yet been attempted.

The wisdom of this world, with its worldly spirit, was the only thing that had overcome the Church, and had carried it into captivity. For in captivity it certainly is, as soon as it is turned into a kingdom of this world ; and a kingdom of this world it certainly is, as soon as worldly wisdom has its power in it. Not a false doctrine, not a bad discipline, not an usurped power, or corrupt practice ever has prevailed, or does prevail in the Church, but has had its whole birth and growth from worldly wisdom.

This wisdom was the great evil root, at which the reforming axe should have been laid, and must be laid, before the Church can be again that virgin spouse of Christ, which it was at the beginning. " If any man," says St. Paul, " will be wise, let him become a fool in this world." This admits of no exception, it is a maxim as universal and unalterable, as that which says, " If any man will follow Christ, let him deny himself." For no man has any more to deny than that, which the wisdom and spirit of this world are, and do in him. For all that is in this world, the lusts of the flesh, the lust of the eye, and the pride of life, are the very things in which alone the wisdom of this world lives, and moves, and has its being. It can be no other, it can rise no higher, nor be any better, than they are and do. For as heavenly wisdom is the whole of all heavenly goodness, so earthly wisdom has the whole evil of all the earthly nature.

St. Paul speaks of a natural man, that cannot know the things of God, but to whom they are mere foolishness. This natural man is only another name for the wisdom of this world; but though he cannot know the things that be of God, yet he can know their names, and learn to speak that which the saints of God have spoken about them. He can make profession of them, be eloquent in their praise, and set them forth in such a desirable view, as shall make them quite agreeable to the children of worldly wisdom. This is the natural man, who having got into the Church, and Church power, has turned the things of God into things of this world. Had this man been kept out of the Church, the Church had kept its first purity to this day; for the fallen state is nothing else but its fall into the hands of the natural man of this world. And when this is the state of the Church, the wisdom of this world (which always loves its own) will be in love with it, will spare no cost to maintain it, will make laws, fight battles in defence of it, and condemn every man as heretical, who dares speak a word against this glorious image of a church, which the wisdom of this world has set up.

This is the great Antichrist, which is neither better nor worse, nor anything else, but the spirit of Satan working against Christ, in the strength and subtlety of earthly wisdom.

If therefore you take anything to be Church reformation, but a full departure from the wisdom of this world, or anything to be your entrance into a salvation church, but the nature, spirit, and works of Christ, become living in you, then, whether Papist or Protestant, reformation or no reformation, all will be just as much good to you, as when a Sadducee turns Publican, or from a Publican becomes a Pharisee. For the

Church of Christ, as it is the door of salvation, is nothing else but Christ Himself.   Christ in us, or we in His Church, is the same thing.   When that is alive wills, and works in you, which was alive in Christ, then you are in His Church ; for that which He was, that must they be who are His.   Without this, it matters not what pale you are in.   To everything but the new creature, Christ says, " I know you not " ; and to every virtue that worldly wisdom puts on, " Get thee behind me, Satan, for thou savourest not the things that be of God."   And the reason why it must be thus, why worldly wisdom, though under a religious form, is and can be nothing else, but that which is called Satan, or Antichrist, is because all that we are, and have from this world, is that very enmity against God, that whole evil which separates us from Him, and constitutes all that death and damnation that belongs to our fallen state.   And so sure as the life of this world is our separation from God, so sure is it that a total departure from every subtlety and prosperity of worldly wisdom, is absolutely necessary to change an evil son of Adam into a holy son of God.

51. Holiness the Sole End of the Church.

And here it is well to be observed, that the Church of Christ is solely for this end, to make us holy as He is holy.   But nothing can do this, but that which has full power to change a sinner into a saint.   And he who has not found that power in the Church, may be assured that he is not yet a true son of that Church. For the Church brings forth no other births, but holy children of God ; it has no other end, no other nature, or work, but that of changing a sinner into a saint. But this can only be done, just as the change of night into day is done, or as the darkness is quite lost in the light. Something as contrary to the whole nature of sin, as light is to darkness, and as powerful over it, as the light is powerful over darkness, can alone do this. Creeds, canons, articles of religion, stately churches, learned priests, singing, preaching, and praying in the best contrived form of words, can no more raise a dead sinner into a living saint, than a fine system of light and colours can change the night into day. For (N.B.) that which cannot help you to all goodness, cannot help you to any goodness, nor can that take away any sin, but that which can take away all sin.

On this ground it is that the apostle said, "Circumcision is nothing, and uncircumcision is nothing"; and on the same ground it must be said that Popery is nothing, and Protestantism is nothing, because all is nothing as to salvation, but a sinner changed into a saint or the apostle's new creature. Call nothing therefore your holy salvation-church, but that which takes away all your sins; this is the only way not to be deceived with the cry about churches, reformations, and divisions.

52. The Mark of true Church Membership being dead unto all sin.

Many are the marks which the learned have given us of the true church; but be that as it will, no man, whether learned or unlearned, can have any mark or proof of his own true church membership, but his being dead unto all sin, and alive unto all righteousness. This cannot be more plainly told us than in

these words of omr Lord, "He that committeth sin,
is the servant of sin"; but surely that servant of sin
cannot at the same time be a living member of
Christ's body, or that new creature, who dwells in
Christ, and Christ in him. To suppose a man born
again from above, yet under a necessity of continuing
to sin, is as absurd as to suppose that the true
Christian is only to have so much of the nature of
Christ born in him, as is consistent with as real a
power of Satan still dwelling in him. "If the Son,"
says Christ, "shall make you free, then ye shall be
free indeed." What is this but saying, if Christ be
come to life in you, then a true freedom from all
necessity of sinning is given to you. Now, if this is
hindered, and cannot come to pass in the faithful
follower of Christ, it must be, because both the
willing and working of Christ in man is too weak
to overcome that, which the devil wills and works in
him. All this absurdity, and even blasphemy, is
necessarily implied in that common doctrine of books
and pulpits, which teaches, that the Christian can
never have done sinning as long as he lives. Well
therefore may Christendom sleep as securely as it
does, under the power of sin, without any thought,
hope, or desire of doing God's will on earth, as it is
done in heaven; without any concern at their not
being pure, as He who has called them is pure, or
walking as He walked.

The Scripture knows no Christian but saints, who
in all things act as becometh saints. But now if the
Scripture saint did not mean a man that eschewed all
evil, and was holy in all his conversation, saint and no
saint would have only such difference, as one carnal

man will always have from another. Preachers and
writers comfort the half Christians with telling them,
that God requires not a perfect, sinless obedience, but
accepts the sincerity of our weak endeavours instead
of it. Here, if ever, the blind lead the blind. For
St. Paul, comparing the way of salvation to a race,
says, "In a race all run, but one obtaineth the prize:
so run that ye may obtain." Now, if Paul had seeing
eyes, must not they be blind who teach, that God
accepts of all that run in the religious race, and
requires not that any should obtain the prize. How
easy was it to see, that the sincerity of our weak
endeavours was quite a different thing from that,
which alone is, and can be the required perfection of
our lives. The first God accepts, that is, bears with.
But why or how ? Not because He seeks or requires
no more, but He bears with them, because, though at
a great distance from, they are, or may be making
towards that perfection, or new creature, which He
absolutely requires, which is the fulness of the stature
of Christ, and is that which Paul says, is the one that
obtains the prize.

The same which Paul says, is said by Christ in
other words, "Strive," says He, "to enter in at the
strait gate." Here our best endeavours are called for,
and therefore accepted by God, and yet at the same
time He adds, "that many shall strive to enter in, but
shall not be able." Why so, whence comes this ? It
is because Christ Himself is the one door into life.
Here the strivers mentioned by Christ, and those
which St. Paul calls runners in a race, are the very
same persons ; and Christ calling Himself the one door
of entrance, is the same thing as when Paul says, that

one only receives the prize, and that one, which alone
obtains the prize, or that enters through the right
door, is that new creature in whom Christ is truly
born.   For whether you consider things natural or
supernatural, nothing but Christ in us, can be our
hope of glory.

53. Of the Necessity of Sinning.

The pleader for imperfection further supports himself by saying, No man in the world, Christ excepted,
was ever without sin.   And so say I too; and with
the apostle I also add, "That if we say we have not
sinned, we make Him a liar."   But then it is as true to
say, that we make Him a liar, if we deny the possibility of our ever being freed from a necessity of
sinning.   For the same word of God says, "If we
confess our sins, He is faithful and just to forgive us
our sins, and (N.B.) to cleanse us from all unrighteousness."

But surely he that is left under a necessity of
sinning as long as he lives, can no more be said to be
cleansed from all unrighteousness, than a man who
must be a cripple to his dying day, can be said to be
cured of all his lameness.   What weaker conclusion
can well be made, than to infer, that because Christ
was the only man that was born and lived free from
sin, therefore no man on earth can be raised to a
freedom from sinning; no better than concluding,
that because the old man is everyone's birth from
Adam, therefore there can be no such thing as a new
man, created unto righteousness, through Christ Jesus,
living and being all in all in Him; no better sense or

logic, than to say, that because our Redeemer could not find us anything else but sinners, therefore He must of all necessity leave us to be sinners.

Of Christ it only can be said, that He is in Himself the true vine; but of every branch that is His, and grows in Him, it must be as truly said, that the life and spirit of the true vine, is the life and spirit of its branches, and that as is the vine, so are its branches. And here let it be well noted, that if the branch has not the life and goodness of the vine in it, it can only be, because it is broken off from the vine, and therefore a withered branch, fit for the fire. But if the branches abide in the vine, then Christ says this glorious thing of them, "Ye shall ask what ye will, and it shall be done unto you" (John xv. 7). The very same glorious thing, which He had before said of Himself, "Father, I thank Thee, that Thou hast heard Me," and (N.B.) "I knew that Thou hearest Me always" (John xi. 41). Now, say that this new creature, who is in such union, communion, and power with God, because Christ is in him, and he in Christ, as really as the vine is in the branches, and the branches in the vine, say that he must be a servant of sin, as long as he lives in this world, and then your absurdity will be as great, as if you had said, that Christ in us must partake of our corruption.

The sober divine, who abhors the pride of enthusiasts, for the sake of humility, says of himself and all men, we are poor, blind, imperfect creatures; all our natural faculties are perverted, corrupted, and out of their right state; and therefore nothing that is perfect can come from us, or be done by us. Truth enough! And the very same truth, as when the apostle says, "The natural man knoweth not the things that be of God. He cannot know them, they are foolishness to Him." This is the man that we all are by nature. But what Scripture ever spoke of, or required any perfect works from this man, any more than it requires the Ethiopian to change his skin? Or what an instructed divine must he be, who considers this old natural man as the Christian, and therefore rejects Christian perfection, because this old man cannot attain to it? What greater blindness, than to appeal to our fallen state, as a proof of a weakness and corruption which we must have, when we are redeemed from it? Is this any wiser, than saying, that sin and corruption must be there where Christ is, because it is there where He is not?

Our Lord has said this absolute truth, that unless we be born again from above, there is no possible entrance into the kingdom of God. What this new birth is in us, and what we get by it, is as expressly told us by His beloved apostle, saying, "That which is born of God sinneth not." This is as true and unalterable, as to say, that which is born of the devil can do nothing else but add sin to sin. To what end do we pray, that "this day we may fall into no sin," if no such day can be had? But if sinning can be made to cease in us for one day, what can do this for us, but that which can do the same to-morrow? What benefit in praying, that "God's will may be done on earth, as it is in heaven," if the earth as long as it lasts must have as many sinners, as it has men upon it? How vainly does the church pray for the baptized person, "that he may have power and strength to have victory, and to triumph against the devil, the world, and the flesh," if this victorious triumph can never be obtained; if notwithstanding this baptism and prayer, he must continue committing sin, and so be a servant of sin, as long as he lives? What sense can there be in making a communion of saints to be an article of our creed, if at the same time we are to believe that Christians, as long as they live, must in some degree or other follow, and be led by the lusts of the flesh, the lust of the eyes, and the pride of life?

54. All Human Imperfection will prevail as much in the Church as in any Human Society, until we know a Continual Inspiration as the power of Deliverance from Sin.

Whence now comes all this folly of doctrines? It is because the church is no longer that spiritual house of God, in which nothing is intended and sought after, but spiritual power and spiritual life, that is become a mere human building, made up of worldly power, worldly learning, and worldly prosperity in gospel matters. And therefore all the frailties, follies, and imperfections of human nature, must have as much life in the church, as in any other human society. And the best sons of such a church, must be forced to plead such imperfections in the members of it, as must be where the old fallen human nature is still alive. And alive it there must be, and its life defended, where the being continually moved, and led by the Spirit of God, is rejected as gross enthusiasm. For nothing but a full birth, and continual breathing and inspiration of the Holy Spirit in the new-born creature, can be a deliverance from all that which is earthly, sensual, and devilish in our fallen nature. This new creature, born again in Christ, of that eternal word which created all things in heaven and on earth, is both the rock and church, of which Christ says, "The gates of hell shall never prevail against it." For prevail they will, and must against everything, but the new creature. And every fallen man, be he where he will, or who he will, is yet in his fallen state, and his whole life is a mere Egyptian bondage, and Babylonian captivity, till the heavenly church, or new birth from above, has taken him out of it.

55. The True Salvation Church.

See how St. Paul sets forth the salvation church, as being nothing else, and doing nothing else, but merely as the mother of this new birth. "Know ye not," says he, "that so many of us as were baptized into Jesus Christ, were baptized into His death? Therefore we are buried with Him by baptism into death, that like as Christ was raised from the dead by the glory of the Father, even so we also should walk in newness of life." Here we have the one true church, infallibly described, and yet no other church, but the new creature. He goes on, "For if we have been planted together in the likeness of His death, we shall be also in the likeness of His resurrection." Therefore to be in Christ, or in His church, belongs to no one, but because the old man is put off, and the new creature risen in Christ, is put on. The same thing is said again in these words,

"Knowing this, that our old man is crucified with
Him, that the body of sin might be destroyed, that
(N.B.) henceforth we should not serve sin"; therefore
the true church is nowhere but in the new creature,
that henceforth sinneth not, nor is any longer a
servant to sin. Away then with all the tedious
volumes of church unity, church power, and church
salvation. Ask neither a Council of Trent, nor a Synod
of Dort, nor an Assembly of Divines, for a definition
of the church. The apostle has given you, not a
definition, but the unchangeable nature of it in these
words. But now "Being made free from sin, and become
servants to God, ye have your fruits unto holiness, and
the end everlasting life." Therefore to be in the true
salvation church, and to be in Christ that new creature
which sinneth not, is strictly the same thing.

What now is become of this true church, or where
must the man go, who would fain be a living member
of it? He need go nowhere; because wherever he is,
that which is to save him, and that which he is to be
saved from, is always with him. Self is all the evil
that he has, and God is all the goodness that he ever can
have; but self is always with him, and God is always
with him. Death to self is his only entrance into
the church of life, and nothing but God can give death
to self. Self is an inward life, and God is an inward
Spirit of life; therefore nothing kills that which must
be killed in us, or quickens that which must come
to life in us, but the inward work of God in the
soul, and the inward work of the soul in God. This
is that mystic religion, which, though it has nothing
in it but the same spirit, that same truth, and that
same life, which always was, and always must be the

religion of all God's holy angels and saints in heaven, is by the wisdom of this world accounted to be madness. As wisely done, as to reckon him mad, who says, that the vanity of things temporal cannot be, or give life to the things that are eternal; or that the circumcision of the flesh is but as poor a thing, as the whetting the knife, in comparison of that inward mystic circumcision of the heart, which can only be done by " that word of God, which is sharper than any two-edged sword, and pierces to the dividing asunder of the soul and spirit" (Heb. iv. 12). Now fancy to yourself a Rabbi-doctor, laughing at this circumcision of the two-edged sword of God, as gospel madness, and then you see that very same Christian orthodoxy, which at this day condemns the inward working life of God in the soul, as mystic madness.

Look at all that is outward, and all that you then see, has no more of salvation in it, than the stars and elements. Look at all the good works you can think of, they have no goodness for you, but when the good Spirit of God is the doer of them in you. For all the outward works of religion may be done by the natural man, he can observe all church duties, stick close to doctrines, and put on the semblance of every outward virtue; thus high he can go. But no Christian, till led and governed by the Spirit of God, can go any higher than this feigned, outward formality of this natural man; to which he can add nothing, but his own natural fleshly zeal in the defence of it. For all zeal must be of this kind, till it is the zeal of that which is born of God, and calls every creature only to that same new birth from above. " My little children," says St. Paul, " of whom I travail again in birth, till Christ be formed in you." This is the whole labour of an apostle to the end of the world. He has nothing to preach to sinners, but the absolute necessity, the true way, and the certain means, of being born again from above.

56. The New Life by the Holy Spirit living in us, the Sole End of Christ's coming.

The eternal Son of God came into the world, only for the sake of this new birth, to give God the glory of restoring it to all the dead sons of fallen Adam. All the mysteries of this incarnate, suffering, dying Son of God, all the price that He paid for our redemption, all the washings that we have from His all-cleansing blood poured out for us, all the life that we receive from eating His flesh, and drinking His blood, have their infinite value, their high glory, and amazing greatness in this, because nothing less than these supernatural mysteries of a God-man, could raise that new creature out of Adam's death, which could be again a living temple, and deified habitation of the Spirit of God.

That this new birth of the Spirit, or the divine life in man, was the truth, the substance, and sole end of His miraculous mysteries, is plainly told us by Christ Himself, who at the end of all His process on earth, tells His disciples, what was to be the blessed, and full effect of it, namely, that the Holy Spirit, the Comforter (being now fully purchased for them) should after His ascension, come in the stead of a Christ in the flesh. "If I go not away," says He, "the Comforter will not come; but if I go away, I will send Him unto you, and He shall guide you into all truth." Therefore all that Christ was, did, suffered, dying in the flesh, and ascending into heaven, was for the sole end, to purchase for all His followers a new birth, new life, and new light, in and by the Spirit of God restored to them, and living in them, as their support, Comforter, and Guide into all truth. And this was His, " Lo, I am with you alway, even unto the end of the world."

ADDITIONAL EXTRACTS.

---

1. The Spirit of the World and the Spirit of God.

(From the Spirit of Prayer, Part 2.)

I shall only add that, from what has been said of the first state and fall of Adam, it plainly follows that the sin of all sins, the heresy of all heresies, is a worldly spirit. We are apt to consider this temper only as an infirmity, or pardonable failure; but it is, indeed, the great apostasy from God and the divine life. It is not a single sin, but the whole nature of all sin, that leaves no possibility of coming out of our fallen state, till it be totally renounced with all the strength of our hearts. Every sin, be it of what kind it will, is only a branch of the worldly spirit that lives in us. Choose any life but the life of God and heaven, and you choose death; for death is nothing else but the loss of the life of God and heaven. The creatures of this world have but one life, and that the life of this world; this is their one life, and their one good. Eternal beings have but one life and one good, and that is the life of God. The spirit of the soul is in itself nothing but a spirit breathed forth from the life of God, and for this only end, that the life of God, the nature of God, the working of God, the tempers of God, may be manifest in it. All the religion of fallen man, all the methods of our redemption, have only this one end, to take from us that strange and earthly life we have gotten by the fall, and to kindle again the life of God and heaven in our souls. It is to take from us entirely the whole spirit of this world. And that for this necessary reason, because all that is in the world, is not of the Father, that is, is not that life, or that spirit of life, which we had from God by our creation; but is of the world, is brought into us by our fall from God into the life of this world. And therefore a worldly spirit is not to be considered as a single sin, or as something that may consist with some real degrees of goodness, but as a real state of death to the kingdom and life of God in our souls.

Hold this therefore as a certain truth, that the heresy of heresies is a worldly spirit. It is the greatest blindness and darkness of our nature, and keeps us in the grossest ignorance of both heaven and hell. For though they are both within us, yet we feel neither the one nor the other so long as the spirit of the world reigns within us. Of all things, therefore, detest the spirit of this world, or there is no help; you must live and die an utter stranger to all that is divine and heavenly. For a worldly spirit can know nothing of God; it can know nothing, feel nothing, taste nothing, delight in nothing, but with earthly senses, and after an earthly manner. For nothing feels, or tastes, or understands, or likes, or dislikes, but the life that is in us. The spirit that leads our life, is the spirit that forms our understanding. All this only to show you the utter impossibility of knowing God and divine truths till your life is divine, and wholly dead to the spirit of the world; since our light and knowledge can be no better or higher, than the state of heart and life is.

If you were to ask me, What is the apostasy of these last days, or whence is all the degeneracy of the present Christian Church? I should place it all in a worldly spirit. If here you see only forms of godliness, there open wickedness; if here superficial holiness, political piety, crafty prudence, there haughty sanctity, partial zeal, envious orthodoxy; all these are only so many proper fruits and forms of the worldly spirit. This is the great net with which the devil becomes a fisher of men. And be assured of this, that every son of man is in this net, till through and by the Spirit of Christ he breaks out of it.

I say the Spirit of Christ; for nothing else can deliver him from it. Trust now to any kind or form of religious observances, to any number of the most plausible virtues, to any kinds of learning, or efforts of human prudence, and then I will tell you what your case will be; you will overcome one temper of the world only and merely by cleaving to another. For nothing leaves the world, nothing renounces it, nothing can possibly overcome it, but singly and solely the Spirit of Christ. Would you further know the evil nature and effects of a worldly spirit, you need only look at the blessed power and effects of the spirit of prayer, for the one goes downward with the same strength as the other goes upward. The spirit of prayer is a pressing forth of the soul out of this earthly life; it is a stretching with all its desire after

the life of God; it is a leaving, as far as it can, all its
own spirit, to receive a Spirit from above, to be one
life, one love, one Spirit with Christ in God.

2. No True Religion but by the Spirit of God.

(*From the Spirit of Prayer, Part 2.*)

Here therefore we are come to this firm conclusion,
that, let religion have ever so many shapes, forms,
reformations, it is no true divine service, no proper
worship of God, has no proper good in it, can do no
good to man, can remove no evil out of man, raise no
divine life in man, but so far as it serves, worships,
conforms, and gives itself up to this operation of the
holy triune God, as living and dwelling in the soul.
Keep close to this idea of religion as an inward
spiritual life in the soul; seek for no good, no comfort,
but in the awakening of all that is holy and heavenly
in your heart; and then, so much as you have of this
inward religion, so much have you of real salvation.
For salvation is only a victory over nature; so far as
you resist and renounce your vain, selfish, and earthly
nature, so far as you overcome all your own natural
tempers of the old man, so far God enters into you,
lives in you and operates; He is in you as the light,
the life, and the Spirit of your soul; and you are in
Him that new creature that worships Him in spirit
and truth.   For divine worship or service is and can
only be performed by being likeminded with Christ;
nothing worships God, but the Spirit of His beloved
Son, in whom He is well pleased.   Look now at anything as religion or divine service, but a strict, unerring

conformity to the life and Spirit of Christ, and then, though every day was full of burnt-offerings, yet you would only be like those religionists, who drew near to God with their lips, but their heart was far from Him. For the heart is always far from God, **unless the Spirit of Christ be alive in it.** But no one has the living Spirit of Christ, but he who in all his conversation walketh as He walked.

All Scripture brings us to the conclusion, that religion is but a dead work, unless it be the work of the Spirit of God; and that sacraments, prayers, singing, preaching, hearing, are only so many ways of being fervent in the spirit, and of giving up ourselves more and more to the inward working, enlightening, quickening, sanctifying Spirit of God within us; and all for this end, that the curse of the fall may be taken from us, that death may be swallowed up in victory, and a real, true Christlike nature formed in us, by the very same Spirit, by which it was formed in the Virgin Mary.

Now, for the true ground, and absolute necessity of this turning wholly to the Spirit of God, you need only know this plain truth; namely, that the Spirit of God, the spirit of Satan, or the spirit of the world, are, and must be, the one or the other of them, the continual leader, guide, and inspirer, of everything that lives in nature. There is no going out of these; the moment you cease to be moved, quickened, and inspired, by God, you are infallibly inspired by the spirit of Satan, or the world, or by both of them. And the reason is, because the soul of man is a spirit, and a life, that in its whole being is nothing else but a birth of God and nature; and therefore every moment of its life must live in conjunction, or union, either with the Spirit of

10

God governing nature, or with the spirit of nature fallen from God, and working in itself. As creatures, we are therefore under an absolute necessity of being under the motion, guidance, and inspiration, of some spirit that is more than our own. All that is put in power is only the choice of our leader; but led and moved we must be, and by that spirit, to which we give up ourselves, whether it be the Spirit of God or the spirit of fallen nature. To seek therefore to be **always under the inspiration and guidance of God's Holy Spirit,** and to act by an immediate inspiration from it, is not proud enthusiasm, but as sober and humble a thought, as suitable to our state, as to think of renouncing the devil and the world. For they never can be renounced by us, but so far as the Spirit of God is living, moving, breathing, in us. And that for this plain reason, because nothing is contrary to the spirit of Satan or the world, nothing works, or can work contrary to it, but the Spirit of heaven.

Hence our Lord said, "He that is not with Me is against Me, and he that gathereth not with Me, scattereth;" plainly declaring, that not to be with Him, and led by His Spirit, is to be led by the spirit of the world, and of Satan. Ask now what hell is? It is nature destitute of the light and Spirit of God, and full only of its own darkness; nothing else can make it to be hell. Ask what heaven is? It is nature quickened, enlightened, blessed, and glorified, by the light and Spirit of God dwelling in it. Here you may see with the utmost clearness, that to look for salvation in anything else, but **the light of God within us, the Spirit of God working in us, the birth of Christ really brought forth within us,** is to be as carnally minded as the Jews were when their hearts were wholly set upon a temporal Saviour. And all for this plain reason, because the soul is a spirit breathed forth from God Himself, which therefore cannot be blessed but by having the life of God in it; and nothing can bring the life of God into it, but only the light and Spirit of God. Upon this ground I stand in the utmost certainty, looking wholly to the light and Spirit of God, for an inward redemption from all the inward evil that is in my fallen nature.

3. The Gospel, a Ministration of the Spirit.

(From the Way of Divine Knowledge.)

Let me now only, before we break up, observe to you the true ground and nature of gospel Christianity; I call it so, by way of distinction from that original universal Christianity, which began with Adam; was the religion of the patriarchs, of Moses and the Prophets, and of every penitent man in every part of the world, that had faith and hope towards God, to be delivered from the evil of this world.

But when the Son of God had taken a birth in and from the human nature, had finished all the wonders that belonged to our redemption, and was sat down at the right hand of God in heaven, then a heavenly kingdom was set up on earth, and the Holy Spirit came down from heaven, or was given to the flock of Christ in such a degree of birth and life, as never was, nor could be given to the human nature, till Christ, the Redeemer of the human nature, was glorified. But when the humanity of Christ, our second Adam, was glorified, and become all heavenly, then the heavenly life, the comfort, and power, and presence of the Holy Spirit, was the gift which He gave to His brethren, His friends and followers, which He had left upon earth.

The Holy Ghost descended in the shape of cloven tongues of fire on the heads of those that were to begin and open the new powers of a divine life set up amongst men. This was the beginning and manifestation of the whole nature and power of gospel Christianity, a thing as different from what was Christianity before, as the possession of the thing hoped for, is different from hope, or deliverance different from the desire or expectation of it. Hence the apostles were new men, entered into a new kingdom, come down from heaven, enlightened with new light, inflamed with new love, and preached not any absent or distant thing, but Jesus Christ, as the wisdom and power of God, felt and found within them, and as a power of God, felt and found within them, and as a power of God ready to be communicated in the same manner, as a new birth from above, to all that would repent and believe in Him. It was to this change of nature, of life and spirit, to this certain, immediate deliverance from the power of sin, to be possessed and governed by gifts and graces of a heavenly life, that men were then called to, as true Christianity. And the preachers of it bore witness, not to a thing that they had heard, but to a power of salvation, a renewal of nature, a birth of heaven, a sanctification of the Spirit, which they themselves had received. Gospel Christianity then stood upon its own true ground; it appeared to be what it was.

And what was it ? Why, it was an awakened divine
life set up amongst men; itself was its own proof;
it appealed to its proper judge, to the heart and
conscience of man, which was alone capable of being
touched with these offers of a new life.

Hence it was, that sinners of all sorts, that felt
the burden of their evil natures, were in a state of
fitness to receive these glad tidings. Whilst the rigid
Pharisee, the orthodox priest, and the rational heathen,
though at enmity with one another, and each proud
of his own distinction, yet all agreed in rejecting and
abhorring a spiritual Saviour, that was to save them
from their carnal selves and the vanity of their own
rational selfish virtues. But when, after a while,
Christianity had lost its first glory, appeared no longer
as a divine life awakened amongst men, and itself was
no longer its own proof of the power and Spirit of
God manifested in it, then heathenish learning, and
temporal power, was from age to age forced to be
called the glory and prosperity of the Church of
Christ; although, in the Revelation of St. John, its
figure is that of a scarlet whore riding upon the beast.

Here therefore, my friend, you are to place the true
distinction of gospel Christianity from all that went
before it, or that is to come up after it It is purely
and solely a divine life awakened, and set up amongst
men, as the effect and fruit of Christ's glorification
in heaven, and has no other promise from Him but
that of His Holy Spirit, to be with it as its light, its
guide, its strength, its comfort, and protection, to the
end of the world. Therefore as gospel Christians, we
belong to the new covenant of the Holy Spirit, which
is the kingdom of God come down from heaven on

the day of Pentecost; and therefore it is, that there
is no possibility of seeing or entering into this new
kingdom, but by being born again by the Spirit. The
apostles and disciples of Christ, though they had been
baptized with water, had followed Christ, heard His
doctrines, and done wonders in His name; yet as then,
stood only near to the kingdom of God, and preached
it to be at hand. They had only seen and known
Christ according to the flesh, had followed Him with
great zeal, but with little and very low knowledge
either of Him or His kingdom; and therefore it was,
that they were commanded to stand still, and not act
as His ministers in His new glorified state, till they
were endued with power from on high: which power
they then received, when the Holy Ghost with His
cloven tongues of fire came down upon them, by which
they became the illuminated instruments, that were to
diffuse the light of an heavenly kingdom over all the
world. From that day began gospel Christianity,
with its true distinction from everything that was
before it; which was the ministration of the Spirit;
and the ministers of it called the world to nothing
but gifts and graces of the same Spirit, to look for
nothing but spiritual blessings, to trust, and hope, and
pray for nothing but the power of that Spirit, which
was to be the one life, and ruling Spirit of this newly-
opened kingdom of God. No one could join himself
to them, or have any part with them, but by dying to
the wisdom and light of the flesh, that he might live
by the Spirit, through faith in Jesus Christ, who had
thus called him to His kingdom and glory. Now this
Christianity is its own proof; it can be proved from
nothing but itself; it wants neither miracles, nor

outward witness; but, like the sun, is its own discoverer.

He that adheres only to the history of the facts, doctrines, and institutions of the gospel, without being born of its spirit, is only such a Christian, and is no nearer to Christ, than the Jew, who carnally adhered to the letter of the Law. They both stand in the same distance from gospel Christianity.

For the truth of Christianity is the Spirit of God living and working in it; and where this Spirit is not the life of it, there the outward form is but like the outward carcass of a departed soul.

For the spiritual life is as much its own proof, as the natural life, and needs no outward or foreign thing to bear witness to it.

4. Reason and Faith.

(From Answer to Dr. Trapp.)

For as the Holy Jesus is but one, the very same yesterday, to-day, and for ever, so His mediatorial, redeeming Spirit in fallen man, is but one, namely, the Spirit of His process, which is one and the same, always working in one and the same manner, where it is submitted to, as well before, as after His incarnation; that is, whether it be called the seed of the woman, or Jesus Christ born of the Virgin Mary. For the one is only the first, the other, the last name of one and the same redeeming Son of God. In the first name, it was the power of Jesus, living in man, in the last name, it was Jesus Himself become man.

Not the smallest spark of goodness ever sprung up in fallen man, no kind of faith, hope, or trust in

God, no patience in adversity, no self-denial, no love of God, or desire of doing His will, no truth of humility, meekness, and compassion, ever did or could work in the heart and spirit of any son of Adam, but solely for this reason, because all these tempers were the spirit of Christ's process, which spirit was inspoken, or ingrafted into fallen man, as soon as God looked with pity, compassion, love, and relief towards Adam and Eve.

For this looking of God with compassion, love, and relief at man, was in truth the very beginning of the incarnation of the Son of God; for it was not something without or separate from God (because God is not without or separate), but it was divine compassion, love, and relief, inwardly working in the inmost ground of the life of man; which blessed power of the redeeming love of God in the soul, was at first called the seed of the woman, till by all kind of evidence it was known and found to be the eternal Son of God born of a virgin.

Now that which Christ did, suffered and obtained in and through His process in the flesh, calling all to turn to God, to deny themselves, to be of His Spirit, to enter into the strictest union with Him, giving heavenly birth and life, and all divine graces to men, and yet only and solely according to their faith in it.

The loss of this faith in the first ages of mankind, gave birth to that which is called the heathen or rational world, for they both began together, and are the same thing, and brought forth a race of people, full of blindness, wickedness, and idolatry. For so far as they departed from faith, as far they fell from

God, under the dominion and government of their reason, passions, and appetites. And thence began the kingdom of this world, and the wisdom of this world, which had, and ever must have, full power over every man, as soon as he ceases to live by faith.

For to live by faith always was, and always will be, living in the kingdom of God; and to live by reason, always was, and always will be, living as a heathen, under the power of the kingdom of this world.

Reasoning instead of faith, brought about the first fall, and dreadful change in the human nature, no less than a real death to God, and the kingdom of heaven. And nothing but faith instead of reasoning, can give any one fallen man, power to become again a son of God. Now to the end of the world, this will be the unalterable difference between faith in God and reasoning about the things of God; they can never change their place, nature, or effects; that which they were, and did to the first man, that they will be, and do to the last.

Faith in God is nothing else but a full adhering to God, and therefore it is one with God, and God with it, and all that is holy, divine, and good may well be found in it.

Reasoning is nothing else but a full adhering to ourselves; and therefore all that is selfish, perverse, corrupt, and serpentine in fallen man, must be kept up and nourished by it.

It matters not in what age, or under what dispensation of God we live, the necessity, the nature, and power of faith is always the same; that simple, illiterate, unreasoning faith, that helped Abraham to right-

eousness, life, and union with God, is the one faith
that alone can be justification, life, and salvation to
Christians; or, which is the same thing, can alone be,
Christ in us, the hope of glory. For faith is nothing
else but so much of the nature, and Spirit of Christ,
born and living in us. " I came," says Christ, " not to
do My own will, but the will of Him that sent Me. My
meat and drink is to do the will of Him that sent Me."
This is the whole nature and perfection of faith. And
as no one but Christ had power to say this of Himself,
so no one can have, or live in this faith, but because
the divine nature of Christ is truly born, and formed
in him, and is become the life of his life, and the spirit
of his spirit.

Again, it matters not, how much the revelations and
precepts of God are increased, since the first single
command given to Adam, for no more is offered to
our reasoning faculty by the whole Bible, than by that
single precept. And the benefit of the whole Bible
is lost to us, as soon as we reason about the nature
and necessity of its commands, just as the benefit of
that first precept was lost in the same way.

" Hath God indeed said, Ye shall not eat of every
tree in the garden?" This was the first essay, or
beginning of reasoning with God. What it was, and
did then, that it will always be, and do. Its nature
and fruits will never be better, or any other, to the
end of the world. And though in these last ages, it
hath passed through all schools of quibbling, and is
arrived at its utmost height of art, subtlety, and pre-
cision of argument, yet as to divine matters, it stands
just where it stood, when it first learnt that logic from
the sepent, which improved the understanding of Eve.

And at this day, it can see no deeper into the things of God, can be no wiser, give no better judgment about them, than that conclusion it at first made, that death could not be in the tree, which was "so good for food, so pleasant to behold, and to be desired for knowledge."

In short, these two, faith and reasoning, have, and always will divide all mankind, from the beginning to the end of the world, into two sorts of men fully distinct from each other.

The faithful, through every age, are of the seed of the woman, the children of God, and sure heirs of His redemption through Jesus Christ.

The reasoners are of the seed of the serpent, they are the heathens through every age, and real heirs of that confusion which happened to be the first builders of the Tower of Babel.

To live by faith, is to be truly and fully in covenant with God; to live by reasoning, is to be merely and solely in compact with ourselves, with our own vanity and blindness.

To live by faith, is to live with God in the spirit and power of prayer, in self-denial, in contempt of the world, in divine love, in heavenly foretastes of the world to come, in humility, in patience, long-suffering, obedience, resignation, absolute trust and dependence upon God, with all that is temporal and earthly under their feet.

To live by reasoning, is to be a prey of the old serpent, eating dust with him, grovelling in the mire of all earthly passions, devoured with pride, embittered with envy, tools and dupes to ourselves, tossed up with false hopes, cast down with vain fears, slaves to all the good and evil things of this world, to-day elated with learned praise, to-morrow dejected at the unlucky loss of it; yet jogging on year after year, defining words and ideas, dissecting doctrines and opinion, setting all arguments and all objections upon their best legs, sifting and refining all notions, conjectures, and criticisms, till death puts the same full end to all the wonders of the ideal fabric, that the cleansing broom does to the wonders of the spider's web, so artfully spun at the expense of its own vitals.

This is the unalterable difference between a life of faith and a life of reasoning in the things of God, the former is from God, works with God, and therefore it saveth, it maketh whole, and all things are possible to it; the latter is from the serpent, works with the serpent, and therefore vain opinions, false judgments, errors, and delusions are inseparable from it, and can only belong to it.

Every scholar, every disputer of this world, nay, every man, has been where Eve was, and has done what she did, when she sought for wisdom that did not come from God. All libraries of the world are the full proof of the remaining power of the first sinful thirst after it: they are full of a knowledge that comes not from God, and therefore proceeds from that first fountain of subtlety that opened her eyes. For as there cannot possibly be any goodness in man, but so far as the divine goodness is living and working good in Him, so that there cannot be any divine truth, or knowledge in man, but so far as God's truth and knowledge is opened, living and working in him, because God alone is all truth, and the knowledge of it.

LETTER I.

5. Of the Inward and Outward Church.

I shall not trouble you with apologising for this long silence, but speak directly to the matters of yours, concerning your difficulty to join in any church communion.

Religion, or church communion is in its true nature, both external and internal, which are thus united, and thus distinguished; the one is the outward sign, the other is the inward truth signified by it: the one never was, nor ever can be, in its true state, without the other.

The inward truth, or church, is regeneration, or the life, Spirit, and power of Christ, quickened and brought to life, in the soul.

The outward sign, or church, is that outward form, or manner of life, that bears full witness to the truth of this regenerated life of Christ, formed or revealed in the soul.

The inward truth gives forth its outward proper manifestations of itself, and these manifestations bring forth the true outward church, and make it to be visible, and outworldly known.

As thus, everything in the inward life, and Spirit, and will of Christ when it becomes living, dwelling, and working in the spirit of our minds, or inward man, is the inward church, or kingdom of God set up within us: and everything in the outward behaviour, and visible conversation of Christ, whilst dwelling amongst men, when practised and followed by us, in the form and manner of our life, makes us the members of that outward church, which he set up in this world.

Inwardly nothing lived in Christ, but the sole will of God, a perpetual regard to His glory, and one continual desire of the salvation of all mankind. When this spirit is in us, then are we inwardly one with Christ, and united to God through Him.

Outwardly Christ exercised every kind of love, kindness, and compassion to the souls and bodies of men; nothing was visible in the outward form of His life, but humility and lowliness of state in every shape; a contented want, or rather total disregard of all worldly riches, power, ease, or pleasure; a continual meekness, gentleness, patience, and resignation, not only to the will of God, but to the haughty powers of the world, to the perverseness, and contradiction of all the evil and malice of men, and all the hardships and troubles of human life: now this, and suchlike outward behaviour of Christ, thus separate from, and contrary to the spirit, wisdom, and way, of this world, was that every outward church, of which he willed all mankind to become visible, and living members. And whoever in the Spirit of Christ, lives in the outward exercise of these virtues, lives as to himself in the highest perfection of church unity, and is the true inward and outward Christian. He is all that he can be, he hath all that he can have, he doth all that he can do, and enjoyeth all that he can enjoy, as a member of Christ's body, or church in this world.

For as Christ was God and man, come down from heaven, for no other end, but fully to restore the union that was lost betwixt God and man, so church unity is, and can be nothing else, but the unity of this, or that man, or number of men with God, through the power and nature of Christ. And therefore it must be the truth, and the whole truth, that nothing more is required, nor will anything else be able, to make anyone a true member of the one Church of Christ, out of which there is no salvation, and in which there is no condemnation, but only and solely his conformity to, and union with the inward Spirit, and outward form of Christ's life and behaviour in this world. This is the one fold under one shepherd; though the sheep are scattered, or feeding in valleys, or on mountains ever so distant, or separate from one another.

On the other hand, not only every unreasonable, unjust action, be it done to whom it will, not only every unkind, proud, wrathful, scornful, disdainful inward thought, or outward behaviour to any person, but every unreadiness to do good of all kinds, to all that we can; every unwillingness to rejoice with them that rejoice, and to weep with them that weep, and love our neighbour as ourselves; every aversion to be inwardly all love, and outwardly all meekness, gentleness, courtesy, and condescension in words and actions towards every creature, for whom Christ died, makes us schismatics, though we be ever so daily gathered together, into one and the same place, joining in one and the same form of creeds, prayers, and praises offered to God, and is truly a leaving, or breaking that church unity, which makes us one with Christ, as our head, and unites us with men, as the members of His body.

That the matter is thus: that the true church unity consists in our walking as Christ walked, fully appears, as from many others, so from these plain

words of our Lord Himself: "Ye are not of this
world, as I am not of this world, but I have chosen
you out of the world." Therefore to have that contrariety to the world, which Christ had, is the one
necessary and full proof of our being His, of our
belonging to Him, and being one with Him.

Again, "Abide in Me, and I in you; if ye abide in
Me, ye shall ask what ye will, and it shall be done to
you. If a man abide not in Me, he is cast forth as a
branch withered, etc. For without Me ye can do
nothing."

Therefore the one true proof of our being living
members of Christ's Church on earth, or only dead
branches, fit for the fire, is nothing else but our being,
or not being, inwardly of that Spirit, and outwardly of
that behaviour, which Christ manifested to the world.

Again, "This is My commandment, that ye love
one another as I have loved you, and by this shall all
men know that ye are My disciples."

Therefore the true and sufficient mark of our outward church membership, is there only, and fully,
outwardly known, and found in every man, where the
outward form of Christ's loving behaviour to all men,
is outwardly seen and known to be in him. These
and the like passages of Christ and His apostles
(though quite overlooked by most modern defenders of
the one church) are the only places that speak home
to the truth, and reality of church unity.

6. Of Spiritual Worship.

It may now be reasonably asked, What is the
divine service, or worship in this church? For every

church must have its divine service and worship, which is the life, strength, and support of it.

It is answered: "That no man can call Christ Lord, but by the Holy Ghost." Therefore nothing is, or can be a divine service in that church, which has Christ for its Lord, but what has the Holy Spirit for its beginner, doer, and finisher. For if it be certain that no one can own Christ as his Lord, but by the Holy Spirit, then it must be equally certain, that no one can serve or worship God through Christ his Lord, in any other way, help, power, or means, but so far as it is all done, in, and by the power of the same Holy Spirit. Whatsoever is born of the flesh is flesh; that is, whatsoever proceeds from, or is done by the natural powers of man, from his birth of flesh and blood, is merely human, earthly, and corrupt, and can no more do anything that is heavenly, or perform a service of worship that is divine, than our present flesh and blood can enter into the kingdom of heaven. Thus saith the apostle, "Ye are not in the flesh, but in the Spirit, if so be, the Spirit of God dwelleth in you. Now if any man hath not the Spirit of Christ, he is none of His." And consequently if not His, he can perform no divine service to Him. Nor can any worship cease to be carnal, or become divine, but by its being all that it is, and doing all that it doth, by the power, and presence of Christ dwelling in our souls, and helping us by His Holy Spirit to cry in truth and reality, Abba Father.

The New Testament never calls us to do, or offer, or allows anything to be done or offered to God, as a divine service, or worship, but what is done in the truth, and reality of faith, of hope, of love, and obedience to God.

But through all the New Testament, no faith, no hope, no love is allowed to be true, and godly, but only that faith, that hope, etc., which solely proceeds from, and is the fruit of the Holy Spirit, living, dwelling, and working in our whole heart, and soul, and spirit.

This spirituality of the Christian religion, is the reason why it was first preached to the world under the name of the kingdom of God, because under this new dispensation, freed from veils, shadows, and figures of good things absent or to come, God Himself is manifested, ruling in us and over us, as an essential light of our lives, as an indwelling word of power, as a life-giving Spirit within us, forming us by a new birth, to become a chosen generation, a royal priesthood, to offer spiritual sacrifices to God, through a new and living way which Christ hath consecrated for us.

If Christ had not only and solely set up this truth of spiritual worship, He had been but another Moses, and though a better teacher, yet still but as a schoolmaster, to some higher state of religion, that was yet wanted, and must be revealed, if so be that man was to be restored to his true state of life, union, and happiness in and with the divine nature. For as God is a Spirit, and our life is spiritual, so no religious worship can be in its true perfection, or bring us into the possession of our highest good, till it raises all that is spirit and life in us, into union and communion with Spirit and life in God.

7. How to Become Spiritual Worshippers.

If it should here be asked, How we are to become and continue worshippers of the Father in spirit and truth ? It is answered: All consists in turning inwards, in attention to that, which is daily and hourly stirring, living, and working in our hearts.

Now though the Scripture nowhere gives this direction in these very words, yet, since it is said in Scripture, that God dwelleth not in temples made with hands, but in the temple of our hearts, since the kingdom of God is said to be within us, and not to come with outward observation, but to be in us, as a secret, living seed of the incorruptible word ; since our hearts is our whole life, and we are said to live, and move, and have our being in God, it is directly telling us that we are to turn inwards, if we would turn to, and find God.

It is directly telling us, that in what manner we are within, as the worship is done there, so is God in such manner within us ; and that He is no otherwise our God, our life, our rest and happiness, than so far as the working of our hearts, is a willing and choosing, a hungering and thirsting to find, feel and enjoy the life-giving power of His holy presence in our souls.

To be inwardly therefore attentive to God, showing the good and the evil, distinguishing the light from the darkness in our own souls ; to listen to the voice of his ever-speaking word, and to watch the movings of his ever-sanctifying Spirit within us, waiting and longing in the spirit of prayer, of faith and hope, of love and resignation, to be inwardly quickened and

revived in the image, and according to the likeness of
that son, in whom He is well pleased, is the worshipping of God with our whole heart and soul, in spirit
and in truth.

It is living to God, in and through the power of
Christ, as He lived; it is praying with Him, and by
His Spirit, that continual prayer which He always
had, whether speaking to the multitude, or healing
their diseases, or alone by Himself in the stillness of
nights, and loneliness of mountains. For this inward
prayer, in which the whole heart, and soul, and spirit,
loves, worships, and applies to a God, not absent or
distant, but to a trinity of goodness and mercy, of
light and love, of glory and majesty, dwelling, and
working within us, willing and desiring to do all that
in the temple of our hearts, which is done and always
doing in His own temple in heaven, is a prayer, that
only needs outward words for the sake of others; and
of which it may be said, as Christ said: "Father, I
knew that Thou always hearest Me, but because of the
people, which stand by, I said it."

I begin to apprehend, worthy sir, that you will
think I am gone too far about, and not come close
enough to the matter in hand. But I hope it is not
so: I have gone through all that I have said, only to
show, that church unity or communion, is not a
matter that depends on any particular society, or outward thing, but is complete, or defective, in such
degree, as we live in unity with, or contrariety to the
inward Spirit and outward example of Christ. For
no union signifies anything to us, or our salvation,
but union with God, through Christ, and nothing
unites us to Christ, or makes us to be His, but His

Holy Spirit dwelling, and working inwardly and outwardly in us, as it did in Him.

This is the only church unity, that concerns the conscience, and when we are in this unity, we are in union with Christ, and with everyone who is united to Him, however distant, or separated from us, by human inclosures.

8. Of the Imperfection of Churches.

I join in the public assemblies, not because of the purity, or perfection of that which is done, or to be found there, but because of that which is meant and intended by them: they mean the holy, public worship of God; they mean the edification of Christians; they are of great use to many people; they keep the world from a total forgetfulness of God; they help the ignorant and letterless to such a knowledge of God, and the Scriptures, as they would not have without them.

And therefore, fallen as these church assemblies are, from their first spiritual state, I reverence them, as the venerable remains of all that, which once was, and will, I hope, be again, the glory of church assemblies, namely, the ministration of the Spirit, and not of the dead letter.

And there are two very great signs of the near approach of this day, in two very numerous, yet very different kinds of people in these kingdoms.

In the one sort, an extraordinary increase of new separations, particularity of opinions, methods, and religious distinctions, is worked up to its utmost height. And we see them almost every day running with eagerness from one method to another, in quest of something, by the help of a new form, which they have not been able to find in the old one.

Now, as the vanity and emptiness of any thing, or way, is then only fully discovered and felt, when it has run all its lengths, and worked itself up to its highest pitch, so that nothing remains untried, to keep up the deceit; so when religious division, strife of opinions, invented forms, and all outward distinctions, have done their utmost, have no further that they can go, nor anything more to try, then is their inevitable fall at hand; and if the zeal was simple and upright, all must end in this full conviction, namely, that vanity and emptiness, burden and deceit, must follow us in every course we take, till we have done with all our own running, to expect all, and receive all from the invisible God dwelling in, and blessing our hearts with all heavenly gifts, by a birth of His eternal, all-creating word, and life-giving Spirit brought forth in our souls.

The other sign I mentioned, is to be found in another kind of a much awakened people, in most parts of these kingdoms, who in the midst of the noise and multiplicity of all church strife, having heard the still, and secret voice of the true Shepherd, are turned inwards, and wholly attentive to the inward truth, spirit, and life of religion, searching after the mystical, spiritual instruction, which leads them from the outward cry, of a Lo here, or there, is Christ, to seek to Him and His redeeming Spirit within them, as the only safe guide from inward darkness to inward light; and from outward shadows into the substantial, ever-enduring truth; which truth is nothing else, but the everlasting union of the soul with God, as its only good, through the Spirit and nature of Christ truly formed and fully revealed in it. But to go no further; I shall only add, that as yet, I know of no better way of thinking or acting, than as above, with regard to the universal fallen state of all churches; for fallen they all are, as certainly as they are divided.

Every church distinction is more or less in the corrupt state of every selfish, carnal, self-willed, worldly-minded, partial man, and is what it is, and acts as it acts, for its own glory, its own interest and advancement, by that same spirit, which keeps the selfish, partial man solely attached to his own will, his own wisdom, self-regard, and self-seeking. And all that is wanting to be removed from every church, or Christian society, in order to its being a part of the heavenly Jerusalem, is that which may be called its own, human will, carnal wisdom, and self-seeking spirit; which is all to be given up, by turning the eyes and hearts of all its members, to an inward adoration, and total dependence upon the supernatural, invisible, omnipresent God of all Spirits; to the inward teachings of Christ, as the power, the wisdom and the light of God, working within them every good, and blessing, and purity, which they can ever receive, either on earth, or in heaven.

Under this light, I am neither Protestant, nor Papist, according to the common acceptation of the words. I cannot consider myself as belonging only to one society of Christians, in separation and distinction from all others. It would be as hurtful to me, if not more so, than any worldly partiality. And therefore as the defects, corruptions, and imperfections which, some way or other, are to be found in all churches, hinder not my communion with that, under which my lot is fallen, so neither do they hinder my being in full union, and hearty fellowship with all that is Christian, holy, and good, in every other church division.

And as I know, that God and Christ, and holy angels, stand thus disposed towards all that is good in all men, and in all churches, notwithstanding the mixture in them, is like that of tares growing up with the wheat, so I am not afraid, but humbly desirous, of living and dying in this disposition towards them.

LETTER II.

9. The First Business of a Clergyman.

It is a great pleasure to me to think (as you say) that my letter to you, will also be to two of your brethren, who stand in the same state of earnestness, to know how to be faithful and useful in their ministry, as you do: I hope God will increase your number.

The first business of a clergyman awakened by God into a sensibility, and love of the truths of the gospel, and of making them equally felt, and loved by others, is thankfully, joyfully, and calmly, to adhere to, and give way to the increase of this new-risen light, and by true introversion of his heart to God, as the sole author of it, humbly to beg of Him, that all that, which he feels a desire of doing to those under his cure, may be first truly and fully done in himself.

Now the way to become more and more awakened, to feel more and more of this first conviction, or work of God within you, is not to reflect and reason yourself into a further and deeper sensibility of it, by finding out arguments to strengthen it in your mind. But the one true way is, in faith and love, to keep close to the presence and power of God, which has manifested itself within you, willingly resigned to, and solely depending upon the one work of His all-creating word, and all-quickening Spirit, which is always more or less powerful in us, according as we are more or less trusting to, or depending upon it.

And thus it is, that by faith we are saved, because God is always ours, in such proportion as we are His; as our faith is in Him, such is His power and presence in us. What an error therefore, to turn one thought from Him, or cast a look after any help but His; for if we ask all of Him, if we seek for all in Him, if we knock only at His own door of mercy in Christ Jesus, and patiently wait and abide there, God's kingdom must come, and His will must be done in us.

For God is always present, and always working towards the life of the soul, and its deliverance from captivity under flesh and blood. But this inward work of God, though never ceasing, or altering, is yet always, and only hindered by the activity of our own nature, and faculties; by bad men through their obedience to earthly passions; by good men through their striving to be good in their own way, by their natural strength, and a multiplicity of seemingly holy labours and contrivances.

Both these sorts of people obstruct the work of God upon their souls. For we can co-operate with

God no other way, than by submitting to the work of God, and seeking, and leaving ourselves to it.

For the whole nature of the fallen soul, consists in its being fallen from God, into itself, into a self-government and activity, under its own powers broken off from God, and therefore dying to self, as well to our reason, as our passions and desires, is the first and indispensable step in Christian redemption, and brings forth that conversion to God, by which Christ becomes formed and revealed in us. And nothing hinders this conversion from being fruitful in all good, and gaining all that we want from God, but the retaining something to dwell in as our own, whether it be earthly satisfactions, or a righteousness of human endeavours.

And therefore all the progress of your first conviction, which by the grace of God you have had from above, and from within, consists in the simplicity of your faith, in adhering to it, as solely the work of God in your soul, which can only go on in God's way, and can never cease to go on in you, any more than God can cease to be that which He is, but so far as it is stopped by your want of faith in it, or trusting to something else along with it. God is found, as soon as He alone is sought; but to seek God alone, is nothing else but the giving up ourselves wholly unto Him. For God is not absent from us in any other respect, than as the spirit of our mind is turned from Him, and not left wholly to Him.

The spirit of faith, which not here, or there, or now and then, but everywhere, and in all things, looks up to God alone, trusts solely in Him, depends absolutely upom Him, expects all from Him, and does all it does for Him, is the utmost perfection of piety in this life. The worship of God in spirit and truth, can go no higher, it does that which is its duty to do; it hath all that it wants, it doth all that it will, it is one power, one spirit, one will, and one working with God. And this is that union or oneness with God, in which man was at first created, and to which he is again called, and will be fully restored by God and man being made one in Christ.

"Stephen was a man full of faith and the Holy Ghost." These are always together, the one can never be without the other.

This was Stephen's qualification for the deaconship, not because of anything high or peculiar in that office, but because the gospel dispensation was the opening a kingdom of God amongst men, a spiritual theocracy, in which as God, and man fallen from God, were united in Christ, so an union of immediate operation between God and man was restored. Hence this dispensation was called, in distinction from all that went before it in outward types, figures, and shadows, a ministration of the Spirit, that is, an immediate operation of the Spirit of God itself in man, in which nothing human, creaturely, or depending upon the power of man's wit, ability, or natural powers, had any place, but all things begun in, and under obedience to the Spirit, and all were done in the power and strength of faith united with God.

Therefore to be a faithful minister of this new covenant between God and man, is to live by faith alone, to act only, and constantly under its power, to desire no will, understanding, or ability as a labourer in Christ's vineyard, but what comes from faith, and full dependence upon God's immediate operation in and upon us.

This is that very thing, which is expressly commanded by St. Peter, saying, " If any man speak, let him speak as the oracles of God, if any man minister, let him do it as of the ability which God giveth." For all which he giveth this reason, which will be a reason as long as the world standeth, namely, " That in all things God may be glorified through Jesus Christ." A plain and sufficient declaration, that where this is not done, there God is not glorified by Christians through Christ Jesus.

God created men and angels solely for the glory of His love; and therefore angels and men, can give no other glory to God, but that of **yielding themselves up to the work of His creating love**, manifesting itself in the several powers of their natural life, so that the first creating love, which brought them into being, **may go on creating, and working in them, according to** its own never-ceasing will, to communicate good for ever and ever. This is their living to the praise and glory of God, namely by owning themselves, in all that they are, and have, and do, to be mere **instruments of His power, presence, and goodness in them, and to them**; which is all the glory they can return to their Creator, and all the glory for which He created them. We can no otherwise give religious glory to God, than by worshipping Him in spirit and in truth, seeing Christ has said, that " the Father seeketh such to worship Him."

But we can no otherwise worship God in spirit and in truth, than as our spirit in truth and reality, **seeks only to, depends only upon, and in all things adores,** the life-giving power of His universal Spirit; as the Creator, upholder, and doer of all that is or can be good, either in time or eternity. For nothing can be good, but that which is according to the will of God; and nothing can be according to the will of God, but that which is done by His own Spirit. This is unchangeable, whether in heaven, or on earth. And this is the one end of all the dispensations of God, however various, towards fallen man, namely, to bring man into an union with God. Comply with all the outward modes and institutions of religion, believe the letter, own the meaning of Scripture facts, symbols, figures, representations, and doctrines, but if you stand in any other use of them, or seek to gain some other good from them, than that of being led out of your own self, from your own will, and own spirit, that the will of God, and the Spirit of God, may do all that is willed, and done by you; however fixed, and steadily you may adhere to such a religion, you stand as fixed and steadily in your own fallen state. For the restoration of fallen man, is nothing else but the restoration of him to his first state, under the will and Spirit of God, in and for which he was created.

You may here perhaps, my dear friend, think that I am speaking too much at large, and not closely enough to the particular matter of your inquiry. But my intention hath been, so to speak to you on this occasion, as to lay a ground for a proper behaviour, under every circumstance of the outward work of your ministry. All things must be set right in yourself first, before you can rightly assist others, towards the attaining to the same state.

10. The first object of Preaching, to stir up the Inward Hearing of the Heart.

Hence you may learn, what you are chiefly to drive at, in all your discourses from the pulpit, and conversation; namely, to turn the attention of men to a power of good, and a power of evil, both of them born and living within them. For in these two things, or states of the soul of every man, lies the full proof of the whole nature, both of the fall, and redemption from it.

Were we not naturally evil, by a birth of evil essentially born and living in us, we should want no redemption; and had we not a birth of something divine in us, we could not be redeemed. Inward evil can only be cured, or overcome by an inward good.

And therefore, as all our salvation is an inward work, or struggle of two births within us, so all the work of your outward instruction, must be to call everyone home to himself, and help every heart to know its own state, to seek, and find, and feel his inward life and death, which have their birth, and growth, and strife against one another, in every son of Adam.

And as this is the one good way of preaching, so it is, of all others, the most powerful, and penetrating into the hearts of all men, let their condition be what it will.

For as these two states are certainly in every soul of man, however blended, smothered, and undistinguished, in their operations for a time, yet they have each of them, in some degree, their hearing ears, which though ever so sunk into dulness, will be forced, more or less, to feel **the power of that voice, which speaks nothing but what is,** and must be in some sort spoken within themselves.

And this is the true end of outward preaching, namely, to give loud notice of the call of God in their souls, which though unheard, or neglected by them, is yet always subsisting within them. It is to make such outward sounds, as may reach and stir up the inward hearing of the heart. It is so to strike all the outward senses of the soul, that from sleeping in an inward insensibility of its own life and death, it may be brought into an awakened and feeling perception of itself, and be forced to know, that the evil of death which is in it, will be its eternal master, unless the good of life that is in it, seeks for victory in the name and power and mediation of Christ, the only Prince of Life, and Lord of Glory, and who only hath the keys of heaven, of death and hell in His hands.

Thus far, and no further, goes the labour and ministry of man, in the preaching of the word, whether it be of Paul, or Cephas.

Hence also you will be well qualified, to open in your hearers, a right sense and knowledge of the truth and reality of every virtue, and every vice, that you are discoursing upon.

For since all that is good and evil, is only so to them, because it lives in the life of their heart; they may easily be taught, that no virtue, whether it be humility, or charity, has any goodness in it, but as it springs in, and from the heart, nor any vice, whether it be pride, or wrath, is any further renounced, than as its power, and place in the heart is destroyed. And thus the insignificancy and vanity of an outward formality, of a virtuous behaviour, and everything short of a new heart, and new spirit in, and through the power of Christ, dwelling vitally in them, may be fully shown to be self-delusion, and self-destruction.

11. The great Work of the Preacher, to lead Men to the Holy Spirit.

Your next great point, as a preacher, should be to bring men to an entire faith in, and absolute dependence upon, the continual power and operation of the Spirit of God in them.

All churches, even down to the Socinians, are forced, in obedience to the letter of Scripture, to hold something of this doctrine.

But as the practice of all churches, for many ages, has had as much recourse to learning, art, and science, to qualify ministers for the preaching of the gospel, as if it was merely a work of man's wisdom, so ecclesiastics, for the most part, come forth in the power of human qualifications, and are more or less full of themselves, and trusting to their own ability, according as they are more or less proficients in science, and literature, languages and rhetoric.

To this, more than to any one other cause, is the great apostasy of all Christendom to be attributed. This was the door, at which the whole spirit of the world, entered into possession of the Christian Church.

Worldly lusts, and interests, vanity, pride, envy, contention, bitterness, and ambition, the death of all that is good in the soul, have now, and always had their chief nourishment, power, and support from a sense of the merit, and sufficiency of literal accomplishments.

Humility, meekness, patience, faith, hope, contempt of the world, and heavenly affections (the very life of Jesus in the soul) are by few people less earnestly desired, or more hard to be practised, than by great wits, classical critics, linguists, historians, and orators in holy orders.

Now to bring man to a right practical knowledge, of that full dependence upon, and faith in the continual operation of the Holy Spirit, as the only raiser and preserver of the life of God in their hearts, and souls, and spirits, it is not enough, you sometimes, or often preach upon the subject, but everything that you inculcate, should be directed constantly to it, and all that you exhort men to, should be required, only as a means of obtaining, and concurring with, that Holy Spirit, which is, and only can be, the life and truth of goodness. And all that you turn them from, should be as from something that resists, and grieves that blessed Spirit of God, which always wills and desires to remove all evil out of our souls, and make us again to be sanctified partakers of the divine nature.

For as they only are Christians, who are born again of the Spirit, so nothing should be taught to Christians, but as a work of the Spirit; nor anything sought, but by the power of the Spirit, as well in hearing, as teaching. It is owing to the want of this, that there is so much preaching and hearing, and so little benefit either of the preacher or hearer.

The labour of the preacher is, for the most part, to display logic, argument, and eloquence, upon religious subjects; and so he is just as much carried out of himself, and united to God by his own religious discourses, as the pleader at the bar is, by his law, and oratory upon right and wrong.

And the hearers, by their regarding such accomplishments, go away just as much helped, to be new men in Christ Jesus, as by hearing a cause of great equity well pleaded at the bar.

Now in both these cases, with regard to preacher and people, the error is of the same kind, namely, a trusting to a power in themselves; the one in an ability, to persuade powerfully; the other in an ability, to act according to that which they hear.

And so the natural man goes on preaching, and the natural man goes on hearing of the things of God, in a fruitless course of life. And thus it must be, so long as either preacher or hearers, seek anything else but **to edify, and be edified in, and through the immediate power and essential presence of the Holy Spirit, working in them.**

The way therefore to be a faithful, and fruitful labourer in the vineyard of Christ, is to stand yourself in a full dependence on the Spirit of God, as having no good power, but as His instrument, and by His influence, in all that you do; and to call others, not to their own strength or rational powers, but to a full hope, and faith of having all that they want, from God alone; not as teaching them to be good by men, but by men and outward instruction, calling them to Himself, to a birth of essential, inherent living goodness, wisdom, and holiness from His own eternal word, and Holy Spirit, living and dwelling in them. For as God is all that the fallen soul wants, so nothing but God alone, can communicate Himself to it; all therefore is lost labour, but the total conversion of the soul, to the immediate essential operation of God in it.

———

LETTER VI.

12. How to be in the Truth?

You tell me, sir, that after a twenty years' zeal, and labour in matters of religion, it has turned to so little account, that you are forced, most earnestly to desire a speedy answer to this question, where you shall go, or what you shall do, to be in the truth?

Religion has no good in it, but as it is the revival, and quickening of that divine nature, which your first father had from God, and nothing can revive it, but that which first created it. God is no otherwise your God, but as He is the God of your life, manifested in it; and He can be no otherwise the God of your life, but as His Spirit is living within you. Satan is no other way knowable by you, or can have any other fellowship with you, but as his evil spirit works, and manifests itself along with the workings of your own spirit. "Resist the devil, and he will flee from you"; but he is nowhere to be resisted, but as a working spirit within you, therefore to resist the devil, is to return from the evil thoughts, and motions that arise within you. "Turn to God, and He will turn to you": but God is an universal Spirit, which you cannot locally turn to, or from; therefore to turn to God, is to cleave to those good thoughts and motions which proceed from His Holy Spirit, dwelling and working in you. This is the God of your life, to whom you are to adhere, listen, and attend, and this is your worshipping Him in spirit and truth. And that is the devil that goeth about as a roaring lion, who has no voice, but that which he speaks within you. Therefore, my friend, be at home, and keep close to that which passes within you, for be it what it will, whether it be a good, in which you delight, or an evil, in which you grieve, you could have neither the one, nor the other, but because a holy God of light and love is essentially dwelling in you. Seek therefore for no other road, nor call anything the way to God, but solely that which is eternal, all-creating, Word, and Spirit, worketh within you. For could anything else have been man's way to God, the Word had not been made flesh.

The last words in your question, namely, to be in the truth, are well expressed, for to be in the truth, is the finished state of man returning to God, thus declared by Christ Himself, " Ye shall know the truth, and the truth shall make you free "; free from the blindness and delusion of your own natural reason, and free from forms, doctrines, and opinions, which others would impose upon you. To be in truth, is to be, where the first holy man was, when He came forth in the image and likeness of God: When he lost Paradise, he lost the truth ; and all that he felt, knew, saw, loved, and liked of the earthly, bestial world, into which he was fallen, was but mere separation from God, a veil upon his heart, and scales upon his eyes. Nothing of his first truth could be spoken of to him, even by God Himself, but under the veil of earthly

things, types, and shadows. The Law was given by
Moses ; but Moses had a veil upon his face, the Law
was a veil, prophecy was a veil, Christ crucified was a
veil, and all was a veil, till grace and truth came by
Jesus Christ, in the power of His Holy Spirit. Therefore to be in the truth, as it is in Jesus, is to be come
from under the veil, to have passed through all those
dispensations, which would never have begun, but that
they might end in a Christ spiritually revealed, and
essentially formed in the soul. So that now, in this
last dispensation of God, which is the first truth itself
restored, nothing is to be thought of, trusted to, or
sought after, but God's immediate, continual working in
the soul, by His Holy Spirit. This, sir, is the where you
are to go, and the what you are to do, to be in the
truth. For the truth as it is in Jesus, is nothing else
but Christ come in the Spirit, and His coming in the
Spirit, is nothing else but the first lost life of God,
quickened, and revealed again in the soul. Everything
short of this, has only the nature of outward type and
figure, which in its best state, is only for a time. If
therefore you look to anything but the Spirit, seek to
any power, but that of the Spirit, expect Christ to be
your Saviour, any other way, than as He is spiritually
born in you, you go back from the grace and truth,
which came by Jesus, and can at best be only a legal
Jew, or a self-righteous Pharisee ; there is no getting
further than these states, but by being born of the
Spirit, living by the Spirit, as His child, His instrument, and holy temple, in which He dwells, and works
all His good pleasure. Drop this full adherence to,
and dependence upon the Spirit, act as in your own
sphere, be something of yourself, and through your own

wisdom, etc., and then, though all that you say, or do,
is with the outward words of the spiritual gospel, and
in the outward practices of the spiritual apostles, yet
for all this, you are but there, where those were, who
worshipped God with the blood of bulls and goats;
for (N.B.) nothing but the Spirit of God, can worship
God in spirit and in truth.

13. How to find the Continual Guidance of the Holy Spirit.

But you will perhaps say, that you are still but
where you were, because you know not how to find the
continual guidance of the Holy Spirit. If you know
how to find your own thoughts, you need not be at a
loss to find the Spirit of God. For you have not a
thought within you, but is either from the good of
the Spirit, or from the evil of the flesh. Now the
good and the evil that are within you, and always
more or less sensible by turns, do each of them teach
you the same work and presence of the Spirit of God.
For the good could not appear as good, nor the evil,
be felt as evil, but because the immediate working of
the Spirit of God creates, or manifests this difference
between them, and therefore be in what state you
will, the power of God's Spirit within you, equally
manifests itself to you; and to find the immediate,
continual, essential working of the Spirit of God
within you, you need only know what good, and evil
are felt within you. For all the good that is in any
thought or desire, is so much of God within you, and
whilst you adhere to, and follow a good thought, you
follow, or are led by the Spirit of God. And on the

other hand, all that is selfish and wicked in thought, or affection, is so much of the spirit of Satan within you, which would not be known, or felt, as evil, but because it is contrary to the immediate continual working of the Spirit of God within you. Turn therefore inwards, and all that is within you, will demonstrate to you, the presence, and power of God in your soul, and make you find, and feel it, with the same certainty, as you find and feel your own thoughts. And what is best of all, by thus doing, you will never be without a living sense of the immediate guidance and inspiration of the Holy Spirit, always equal to your dependence upon it, always leading you from strength to strength in your inward man, till all your knowledge of good and evil, is become nothing else, but a mere love of the one, and mere aversion to the other. For the one work of the Spirit of God, is to distinguish the good, and evil, that is within you, not as in notion, but by affection; and when you are wholly given up to this new-creating work of God, so as to stay your mind upon it, abide with it, and expect all from it, this, my friend, will be your returning to the rock, from whence you were hewn, your drinking at the fountain of living water, your walking with God, your living by faith, your putting on Christ, your continual hearing the Word of God, your eating the bread that came down from heaven, your supping with Christ, and following the Lamb wherever He goeth.

For all these seeming different things, will be found in every man, according to his measure, who is wholly given up to, and depending upon the blessed work of God's Spirit in his soul.

14. Redemption, the restoration of the lost knowledge of God, as essentially living and working in the Soul.

But your mistake, and that of most Christians, lies in this : you would be good by some outward means, you would have methods, opinions, forms, and ordinances of religion, alter and raise your fallen nature, and create in you a new heart, and a new spirit, that is to say, you would be good in a way that is altogether impossible, for goodness cannot be brought into you from without, much less by anything that is creaturely, or the action of man ; this is as impossible, as for the flesh to sanctify the spirit, or for things temporal to give life to things that are eternal.

The image and likeness of Father, Son, and Holy Ghost, are in every man, antecedent to every outward work, or action that can proceed from him ; it is God thus within him, that is the sole cause that anything can be called godly, that is done, observed, or practised by him.   If it were not so, man would only have his being from God, but his goodness from himself.

All man's outward good works, are only like his outward good words ; he is not good, because he is frequent in the use of them, they bring no goodness into him, nor are of any worth in themselves, but as a good and godly spirit speaks forth itself in the sound of them.   This is the case of every outward, creaturely thing, or work of man, be it of what kind it will, either hearing, praying, singing, or preaching, etc., or practising any outward rules, and observances ; they have only the goodness of the outward Jew, nay, are as vain, as sounding brass, and tinkling cymbals, unless they be solely the work, and fruits of the Spirit of God: for the divine nature, is that alone, which can be the power to any good work, either in man, or angel.

When a man, first finds himself stirred up with religious zeal, what does he generally do? He turns all his thoughts outwards, he runs after this, or that man, he is at the beck of every new opinion, and thinks only of finding the truth, by resting in this, or that method, or society of Christians. Could he find a man, that did not want to have him of his party, and opinion, that turned him from himself, and the teaching of man, to a God, not as historically read of in books, or preached of in this, or that society, but to a God essentially living and working in every soul, him he might call a man of God; as leading him from himself to God, as saving him from many vain wanderings, from fruitless searches into a Council of Trent, a Synod of Dort, an Augsberg Confession, an Assembly's Catechism, or a Thirty-nine Articles. For had he an hundred articles, if they were anything else but an hundred calls to a Christ come in the Spirit, to a God within him, as the only possible light, and teacher of his mind, it would be a hundred times better for him, to be without them. For all man's blindness and misery lies in this, that he has lost the knowledge of God, as essentially living within him, and by falling under the power of an earthly, bestial life, thinks only of God, as living in some other world, and so seeks only by notions, to set up an image of an absent God, instead of worshipping the God of life, and power, in whom he lives, moves, and has his being. Whoever therefore teaches you to expect great things from this, or that sort of opinions, or calls you to anything as

saving, and redeeming, but the manifestation of God in
your own soul, through a birth of the holy nature of
Christ within you, is totally ignorant of the whole
nature, both of the fall, and redemption of man. For
the first is nothing else, or less, than a death to the
divine life, or Christlike nature, which lived in the
first man; and the other, is nothing else, but Christ
new-born, formed, and revealed again in man, as He
was at the first. These two great truths, are the most
strongly asserted by Christ, saying, " If any man will
be My disciple, let him deny himself, take up his cross
daily, and follow Me." Let him " deny himself," is
the fullest declaration, and highest proof, that he has
lost his first divine and heavenly nature, that he is
not that self, which came first from God, or he could
not be called to deny it. Say, if you will, that he
has not lost that first heavenly life in God, and then
you must say, that our Lord calls him to deny, crucify,
and renounce that holy, and godlike self, which was
the first gift of God to him.

Christ and His apostles taught nothing but death,
and denial to all self, and the impossibility of having
any one divine temper, but through faith, and hope of
a new nature, not " born of blood, nor of the will of the
flesh, nor of the will of man, but of God."

To speak of the operation of the Holy Spirit, as only
an assistance, or an occasional assistance, is as short of
the truth, as to say, that Christ shall only assist the
resurrection, of our bodies. For not a spark of any
divine virtue can arise up in us, but what must wholly
and solely be called forth, by that same power, which
alone can call our dead bodies, out of the dust and
darkness of the grave.

If you turn to your own strength, to have Christian piety, and goodness; or are so deceived, as to think, that learning, or logical abilities, critical acuteness, skill in languages, church systems, rules and orders, articles and opinions, are to do that for you, which the Spirit of Christ did, and only could do for the first Christians; your diligent reading the history of the gospel, will leave you as poor, and empty and dead to the divine life, as if you had been only a diligent reader of the history of all the religions in the world. But if all that you trust to, long after, and depend upon, is that Holy Spirit, which alone made the Scripture saints able to call Jesus Lord; if this be your one faith, and one hope, the divine life, which died in Adam, will find itself alive again in Christ Jesus. And be assured, that nothing but this new birth, can be the gospel Christian, because nothing else can possibly love, like, do, and be that, which Christ preached in His divine Sermon on the Mount. And be assured also, that when the Spirit of Christ, is the Spirit that ruleth in you, there will be no hard sayings in the gospel; but all that the heavenly Christ taught in the flesh, will be as meat and drink to you, and you will have no joy, but in walking, as He walked, in saying, loving, and doing, that which He said, loved, and did. And indeed, how can it be otherwise? How can notions, doctrines, and opinions about Christ, what He was, and did, make you in Him a new creature? Can anyone be made a Samson, or a Solomon, by being well versed in the history of what they were, said or did?

Ask then, my friend, no more, where you shall go, or what you shall do, to be in the truth; for you can

have the truth, nowhere, but in Jesus, nor in Him,
any further, than as His whole nature, and Spirit is
born within you.

———

LETTER X.

15. Of a Sense of Sin.

You seem to yourself to be all infatuation and
stupidity, because your head, and your heart are so
contrary, the one delighting in heavenly notions, the
other governed by earthly passions, and pursuits.   It
is happy for you, that you know and acknowledge
this : for only through this truth, through the full
and deep perception of it, can you have any entrance,
or so much as the beginning of an entrance into the
liberty of the children of God.   God is in this respect
dealing with you, as He does with those, whose darkness is to be changed into light.   Which can never be
done, till you fully know (1) the real badness of your
own heart, and (2) your utter inability to deliver
yourself from it, by any sense, power, or activity of
your own mind.

And were you in a better state, as to your own
thinking, the matter would be worse with you.   For
the badness in your heart, though you had no sensibility of it, would still be there, and would only be
concealed, to your much greater hurt.   For there it
certainly is, whether it be seen and found, or not, and
sooner or later, must show itself in its full deformity,
or the old man may never die the death which is due
to him, and must be undergone, before the new man
in Christ can be formed in us.

All that you complain of in your heart is common to man, as man. There is no heart that is without it. And this is the one ground, why every man, as such, however different in temper, complexion, or natural endowments from others, has one and the same full reason, and absolute necessity, of being born again from above.

Flesh and blood, and the spirit of this world, govern every spring in the heart of the natural man. And therefore you can never enough adore that ray of divine light, which breaking in upon your darkness, has discovered this to be the state of your heart, and raised only those faint wishes that you feel to be delivered from it.

For faint as they are, they have their degree of goodness in them, and as certainly proceed solely from the goodness of God working in your soul, as the first dawning of the morning, is solely from, and wrought by the same sun, which helps us to the noonday light. Firmly, therefore, believe this, as a certain truth, that the present sensibility of your incapacity for goodness, is to be cherished as a heavenly seed of life, as the blessed work of God in your soul.

Could you like anything in your own heart, or so much as fancy any good to be in it, or believe that you had any power of your own to embrace and follow truth, this comfortable opinion, so far as it goes, would be your turning away from God and all goodness, and building iron walls of separation betwixt God and your soul.

For conversion to God, only then begins to be in truth, and reality, when we see nothing that can give us the least degree of faith, of hope, of trust, or comfort in anything, that we are of ourselves.

To see vanity of vanities in all outward things, to loathe and abhor certain things, is indeed something, but yet as nothing, in comparison of seeing and believing the vanity of vanities within us, and ourselves as utterly unable to take one single step in true goodness, as to add one cubit to our stature.

Under this conviction, the gate of life is opened to us. And therefore it is, that all the preparatory parts of religion, all the various proceedings of God either over our inward, or outward state, setting up, and pulling down, giving, and taking away, light, and darkness, comfort, and distress, as independently of us, as He makes the rain to descend, and the winds to blow, are all of them for this only end, to bring us to this conviction, that all that can be called life, good, and happiness, is to come solely from God, and not the smallest spark of it from ourselves. When man was first created, all the good that he had in him was from God alone. N.B. This must be the state of man for ever. From the beginning of time through all eternity, the creature can have no goodness, but that which God creates in it.

Our first created goodness is lost, because our first father departed from a full, absolute dependence upon God. For a full, continual, unwavering dependence upon God, is that alone which keeps God in the creature, and the creature in God.

Our lost goodness can never come again, or be found in us, till by a power from Christ living in us, we are brought out of ourselves, and all selfish truths, into that full and blessed dependence upon God, in which our first Father should have lived.

What room now, my dear friend, for complaint at the sight, sense, and feeling of your inability to make yourself better than you are ? Did you want this sense, every part of your religion would only have the nature and vanity of idolatry. For you cannot come unto God, you cannot believe in Him, you cannot worship Him in spirit and truth, till He is regarded as the only giver, and you yourself as nothing else but the receiver of every heavenly good, that can possibly come to life in you.

Can it trouble you, that it was God that made you, and not you yourself ? Yet this would be as unreasonable, as to be troubled that you cannot make heavenly affection, or divine powers to spring up, and abide in your soul.

God must for ever be God alone ; heaven, and the heavenly nature are His, and must for ever and ever be received only from Him, and for ever and ever be only preserved, by an entire dependence upon, and trust in Him. Now as all the religion of fallen man, fallen from God into himself, and the spirit of this world, has no other end, but to bring us back to an entire dependence upon God ; so we may justly say, Blessed is that light, happy is that conviction, which brings us into a full and settled despair, of ever having the least good from ourselves.

Then we are truly brought, and laid at the gate of mercy : at which gate, no soul ever did, or can lay in vain.

A broken and contrite heart God will not despise. That is, God will not, God cannot pass by, overlook,

or disregard it.   But the heart is then only broken
and contrite, when all its strongholds are broken
down, all false coverings taken off, and it sees, with
inwardly opened eyes, everything to be bad, false, and
rotten, that does, or can proceed from it as its own.

But you will perhaps say, that your conviction is
only an uneasy sensibility of your own state, and has
not the goodness of a broken and contrite heart in it.

Let it be so, yet it is rightly in order to it, and it
can only begin, as it begins at present in you.   Your
conviction is certainly not full and perfect; for if it
was, you would not complain, or grieve at inability to
help or mend yourself, but would patiently expect,
and only look for help from God alone.

But whatever is wanting in your conviction, be it
what it will, it cannot be added by yourself, nor come
any other way, than as the highest degree of the
divine life can come into it.

Know therefore your want of this, as of all other
goodness.   But know also at the same time, that it
cannot be had through your own willing and running,
but through God that showeth mercy; that is to say,
through God who giveth us Jesus Christ.   For Jesus
Christ is the one only mercy of God to all the fallen
world.

Now if all the mercy of God is only to be found in
Christ Jesus, if He alone can save us from our sins; if
He alone has power to heal all our infirmities, and
restore original righteousness, what room for any other
pains, labour, or inquiry, but where, and how Christ
is to be found.

It matters not what our evils are, deadness, blindness, infatuation, hardness of heart, covetousness,

wrath, pride, and ambition, etc., our remedy is always one and the same, always at hand, always certain and infallible. Seven devils are as easily cast out by Christ as one. He came into the world, not to save from this, or that disorder, but to destroy all the power and works of the devil in man.

16. How Christ is to be Found.

If you ask where, and how Christ is to be found ? I answer in your heart, and by your heart, and nowhere else, nor by anything else.

But you will perhaps say, it is your very heart that keeps you a stranger to Christ, and Him to you, because your heart is all bad, as unholy as a den of thieves.

I answer, that the finding this to be the state of your heart, is the real finding of Christ in it.

For nothing else but Christ can reveal, and make manifest the sin and evil in you. And He that discovers, is the same Christ that takes away sin. So that, as soon as complaining guilt, sets itself before you, and will be seen, you may be assured, that Christ is in you of a truth.

For Christ must first come as a discoverer and reprover of sin. It is the infallible proof of His holy presence within you.

Hear Him, reverence Him, submit to Him as a discoverer and reprover of sin. Own His power and presence in the feeling of your guilt, and then He that wounded, will heal, He that found out the sin, will take it away, and He who showed you your den of thieves, will turn it into a holy temple of Father, Son, and Holy Ghost.

And now, sir, you may see, that your doubt and inquiry of me, whether your will was really free, or not, was groundless.

You have no freedom, or power of will, to assume any holy temper, or take hold of such degrees of goodness, as you have a mind to have. For nothing is, or ever can be goodness in you, but the one life, light, and Spirit of Christ revealed, formed, and begotten in your soul. Christ in us, is our only goodness, as Christ in us, is our hope of glory. But Christ in us is the pure free gift of God to us.

But you have a true and full freedom of will and choice, either to leave, and give up your helpless self to the operation of God on your soul, or to rely upon your own rational industry, and natural strength of mind. This is the truth of the freedom of your will, in your first setting out, which is a freedom that no man wants, or can want so long as he is in the body. And every unregenerate man has this freedom.

If therefore you have not that which you want to have of God, or are not that which you ought to be in Christ Jesus, it is not because you have no free power of leaving yourself in the hands, and under the operation of God, but because the same freedom of your will, seeks for help where it cannot be had, namely, in some strength and activity of your own faculties.

Of this freedom of will it is said, " According to thy faith, so it be done unto thee "; that is to say, according as thou leavest and trustest thyself to God, so will His operation be in thee.

This is the real, great magic power of the first

turning of the will; of which it is truly said, that it always hath that which it willeth, and can have nothing else.

When this freedom of the will wholly leaves itself to God, saying, not mine, but Thy will be done, then it hath that, which it willeth. The will of God is done in it. It is in God. It hath divine power. It worketh with God, and by God, and comes at length to be that faith, which can remove mountains; and nothing is too hard for it.

And thus it is, that every unregenerate son of Adam hath life and death in his own choice, not by any natural power of taking which he will, but by a full freedom, either of leaving, and trusting himself to the redeeming operation of God, which is eternal life, or of acting according to his own will and power in flesh and blood, which is eternal death.

And now, my dear friend, let me tell you, that as here lies all the true and real freedom, which cannot be taken from you, so in the constant exercise of this freedom, that is, in a continual leaving yourself to, and depending upon the operation of God in your soul, lies all your road to heaven. No divine virtue can be had any other way.

All the excellency and power of faith, hope, love, patience, and resignation, etc., which are the true and only graces of the spiritual life, have no other root or ground, but this free, full leaving of yourself to God, and are only so many different expressions of your willing nothing, seeking nothing, trusting to nothing, but the life-giving power of His holy presence in your soul.

To sum up all in a word. Wait patiently, trust

humbly, depend only upon, seek solely to a God of light and love, of mercy and goodness, of glory and majesty, ever dwelling in the inmost depth and spirit of your soul. There you have all the secret, hidden, invisible upholder of all the creation, whose blessed operation will always be found by a humble, faithful, loving, calm, patient introversion of your heart to Him, who has His hidden heaven within you, and which will open itself to you, as soon as your heart is left wholly to His eternal ever-speaking word, and ever-sanctifying Spirit within you.

Beware of all eagerness and activity of your own natural spirit and temper. Run not in any hasty ways of your own. Be patient under the sense of your own vanity and weakness; and patiently wait for God to do His own work, and in His own way. For you can go no faster, than a full dependence upon God can carry you.

Nothing that you do, or practise as a good to yourself, and other people, is in its proper state, grows from its right root, or reaches its true end, till you look for no willing, nor depend upon any doing that which is good, but by Christ, the wisdom and power of God, living in you. I caution you against all eagerness and activity of your own spirit, so far as it leads you to seek, and trust to something that is not God, and Christ within you.

I recommend to you stillness, calmness, patience, etc., not to make you lifeless, and indifferent about good works, or indeed with any regard to them, but solely with regard to your faith, that it may have its proper soil to grow in, and because all eagerness, restlessness, haste, and impatience, either with regard to

God, or ourselves, are not only great hindrances, but real defects of our faith and dependence upon God.

Lastly, be courageous then, and full of hope, not by looking at any strength of your own, or fancying that you now know how to be wiser in yourself, than you have hitherto been; no, this will only help you to find more and more defects of weakness in yourself; but be courageous in faith, and hope, and dependence upon God. And be assured, that the one infallible way to all that is good, is never to be weary in waiting, trusting, and depending upon God manifested in Christ Jesus.

March 20, 1756.

LETTER XI.

17. Man's Two Enemies: Self and the World.

Let every evil, whether inward, or outward, only teach you this truth, that man has infallibly lost his first divine life in God; and that no possible comfort, or deliverance is to be expected, but only in this one thing, that though man had lost his God, yet God is become man, that man may be again alive in God, as at the first. For all the misery and distress of human nature, whether of body or mind, is wholly owing to this one cause, that God is not in man, nor man in God, as the state of his nature requires; it is, because man has lost that first life of God in his soul, in and for which he was created. He lost this light, and Spirit, and life of God, by turning his will, imagination, and desire, into a tasting and sensibility of the good and evil of this earthly, bestial world.

Now here are two things raised up in man, instead of the life of God: first, self, or selfishness, brought forth by his choosing to have a wisdom of his own, contrary to the will and instruction of his Creator. Secondly, an earthly, bestial, mortal life and body, brought forth by his eating that fruit, which was poison to his paradisaical nature. Both these must therefore be removed; that is, a man must first totally die to self, and all earthly desires, views, and intentions, before he can be again in God, as his nature and first creation requires.

But now if this be a certain and immutable truth, that man, so long as he is a selfish, earthly-minded creature, must be deprived of his true life, the life of God, the Spirit of Heaven in his soul; then how is the face of things changed! For then, what life is so much to be dreaded, as a life of worldly ease and prosperity? What a misery, nay what a curse, is there in everything that gratifies and nourishes our self-love, self-esteem, and self-seeking? On the other hand, what happiness is there in all inward and outward troubles and vexations, when they force us to feel and know the hell that is hidden within us, and the vanity of everything without us, when they turn our self-love into self-abhorrence, and force us to call upon God to save us from ourselves, to give us a new life, new light, and new spirit in Christ Jesus.

18. The Infinite Love of God.

Only let your present and past distress make you feel and acknowledge this twofold great truth: first, that in and of yourself, you are nothing but darkness, vanity, and misery; secondly, that of yourself, you can no more help yourself to light and comfort, than you can create an angel. People at all times can seem to assent to these two truths; but then it is an assent that has no depth or reality, and so is of little or no use; but your condition has opened your heart for a deep and full conviction of these truths. Now give way, I beseech you, to this conviction, and hold these two truths, in the same degree of certainty as you know two and two to be four, and then you are with the prodigal come to yourself, and above **half your work is done.**

Being now in full possession of these two truths, feeling them in the same degree of certainty, as you feel your own existence, you are, under this sensibility, to give up yourself absolutely and entirely to God in Christ Jesus, as into the hands of infinite love; firmly believing this great and infallible truth, that God has no will towards you, but that of infinite love, and infinite desire to make you a partaker of His divine nature; and that it is as absolutely impossible for the Father of our Lord Jesus Christ to refuse all that good and life and salvation which you want, as it is for you to take it by your own power.

O drink deep of this cup! for the precious water of eternal life is in it. Turn unto God with this faith; cast yourself into this abyss of love; and then you will be in that state the prodigal was in, when he said, "I will arise and go to my father, and will say unto him, Father, I have sinned against heaven, and before thee, and am no more worthy to be called thy son;" and all that will be fulfilled in you, which is related of him.

Make this, therefore, the twofold exercise of your

heart; now, bowing yourself down before God, in the deepest sense and acknowledgment of your own nothingness and vileness; then, looking up unto God in faith and love, consider him as always extending the arms of His mercy towards you, and full of an infinite desire to dwell in you, as He dwells in angels in heaven. Content yourself with this inward and simple exercise of your heart, for a while; and seek, or like nothing in any book, but that which nourishes and strengthens this state of your heart.

" Come unto Me," says the Holy Jesus, " all ye that labour, and are heavy laden, and I will refresh you." Here is more for you to live upon, more light for your mind, more of unction for your heart, than in volumes of human instruction. Pick up the words of the Holy Jesus, and beg of Him to be the light and life of your soul; love the sound of His name; for Jesus is the love, the sweetness, the compassionate goodness, of the Deity itself; which became man, that so men might have power to become the sons of God. Love and pity and wish well to every soul in the world; dwell in love, and then you dwell in God; hate nothing but the evil that stirs in your own heart.

Teach your heart this prayer, till your heart continually saith, though not with outward words: " O Holy Jesus : meek lamb of God ! Bread that came down from heaven ! Light and life of all holy souls ! help me to a true and living faith in Thee. O do Thou open Thyself within me, with all Thy holy nature, spirit, tempers, and inclinations, that I may be born again of Thee, in Thee a new creature, quickened and revived, led and governed by Thy Holy Spirit."

Prayer so practised, becomes the life of the soul

and the true food of eternity. Keep in this state of application to God; and then you will infallibly find it to be the true way of rising out of the vanity of time, into the riches of eternity.

Do not expect, or look, for the same degrees of sensible fervour. The matter lies not there. Nature will have its share; but the ups and downs of that are to be overlooked. Whilst your will-spirit is good, and set right, the changes of creaturely fervour lessen not your union with God. It is the abyss of the heart, an unfathomable depth of eternity within us, as much above sensible fervour, as heaven is above earth; it is this that works our way to God, and unites with heaven. This abyss of the heart, is the divine nature and power within us, which never calls upon God in vain; but whether helped or deserted by bodily fervour, penetrates through all outward nature, as easily and effectually as our thoughts can leave our bodies, and reach into the regions of eternity.

The poverty of our fallen nature, the depraved workings of flesh and blood, the corrupt tempers of our polluted birth in this world, do us no hurt, so long as the spirit of prayer works contrary to them, and longs for the first birth of the light and spirit of heaven. All our natural evil ceases to be our own evil, as soon as our will-spirit turns from it; it then changes its nature, loses all its poison and death, and only becomes our holy cross, on which we happily die from self and this world into the kingdom of heaven.

Would you have done with error, scruple, and delusion? Consider the Deity to be the greatest love, the greatest meekness, the greatest sweetness, the eternal unchangeable will to be a good and blessing to every creature; and that all the misery, darkness, and death of fallen angels and fallen men, consist in their having lost their likeness to this divine nature. Consider yourself, and all the fallen world, as having nothing to seek or wish for, but by the spirit of prayer to draw into the life of your soul, rays and sparks of this divine, meek, loving, tender nature of God. Consider the holy Jesus as the gift of God to your soul, to begin and finish the birth of God and heaven within you, in spite of every inward and outward enemy. These three infallible truths, heartily embraced, and made the nourishment of your soul, shorten and secure the way to heaven, and leave no room for error, scruple, or delusion.

Expect no life, light, strength, or comfort, but from the Spirit of God, dwelling and manifesting His own goodness in your soul. The best of men, and the best of books, can only do you good, so far as they turn you from themselves, and every human thing, to seek, and have, and receive every kind of good from God alone; not a distant, or an absent God, but a God living, moving, and always working in the spirit and heart of your soul.

They never find God, who seek for Him by reasoning and speculation; for since God is the highest Spirit, and the highest life, nothing but a like spirit, and a like life, can unite with him, find or feel, or know anything of Him. Hence it is, that faith, and hope, and love, turned towards God, are the only possible, and also infallible means of obtaining a true and living knowledge of Him. And the reason is plain, it is because by these holy tempers, which are the workings of spirit and life within us, we seek the God of life where He is, we call upon Him with His own voice, we draw near to Him by His own Spirit; for nothing can breathe forth faith, and love, and hope to God, but that spirit and life which is of God, and which therefore through flesh and blood thus presses towards him, and readily unites with him.

There is not a more infallible truth in the world than this, that neither reasoning nor learning can ever introduce a spark of heaven into our souls. But if this be so, then you have nothing to seek, nor anything to fear, from reason. Life and death are the things in question: they are neither of them the growth of reasoning or learning, but each of them is a state of the soul, and only thus differ, death is the want, and life the enjoyment of its highest good. Reason, therefore, and learning, have no power here; but only by their vain activity to keep the soul insensible of that life and death, one of which is always growing up in it, according as the will and desire of the heart worketh. Add reason to a vegetable, and you add nothing to its life or death. Its life and fruitfulness lieth in the soundness of its root, the goodness of the soil, and the riches it derives from air and light. Heaven and hell grow thus in the soul of every man: his heart is his root; if that is turned from all evil, it is then like the plant in a good soil; when it hungers and thirsts after the divine life, it then infallibly draws the light and Spirit of God into it, which are infinitely more ready and willing to live and fructify in the soul, than light and air to enter into the plant, that hungers after them. For the soul hath its breath, and being, and life, for no other end, but that the **triune** God may manifest the riches and power of His own life in it.

19. Of giving up all for God.

Thus hunger is all, and in all worlds, everything lives in it, and by it; nothing else eats, or partakes of life; and everything eats according to its own hunger. Everything hungers after its own mother, that is, everything has a natural magnetic tendency to partake of that from which it had its being, and can only find its rest in that from whence it came. Dead as well as living things bear witness to this truth: the stones fall to the earth, the sparks fly upwards, for this only reason, because everything must tend towards that from whence it came.

Were not angels and the souls of men breathed forth from God, as so many real offsprings of the divine nature, it would be as impossible for them to have any desire of God, as for stones to go upwards, and the flame downwards. Thus you may see, and feel, that the spirit of prayer not only proves that you came from God, but is your certain way of returning to Him.

When, therefore, it is the one ruling, never-ceasing desire of our hearts, that God may be the beginning and end, the reason and motive, the rule and measure, of our doing, or not doing, from morning to night; then everywhere, whether speaking or silent, whether inwardly or outwardly employed, we are equally **offered up to the eternal Spirit**, have our life in Him and from Him, and are united to Him, by that spirit of prayer, which is the comfort, the support, the strength and security of the soul, travelling by the help of God, through the vanity of time into the riches of eternity. For this spirit of prayer, let us willingly give up all that we inherit from our fallen father, to be all hunger and thirst after God; and to have no thought or care, but how to be wholly His devoted instruments; everywhere, and in everything, His adoring, joyful, and thankful servants. Have your eyes shut, and ears stopped to everything, that is not a step in that ladder that reaches from earth to heaven.

Reading is good, hearing is good, conversation and meditation are good; but then they are only good at times and occasions, in a certain degree; and must be used and governed, with such caution, as we eat and drink, and refresh ourselves, or they will bring forth in us the fruits of intemperance. But the spirit of prayer is for all times, and all occasions; it is a lamp that is to be always burning, a light to be ever shining; everything calls for it, everything is to be done in it, and governed by it; because it is, and means, and wills nothing else, but the whole totality of the soul, not doing this or that, but wholly, incessantly given up to God, to be where, and what, and how He pleases.

This state of absolute resignation, naked faith, and pure love of God, is the highest perfection, and most purified life of those, who are born again from above, and through the divine power become sons of God. And it is neither more nor less, than what our blessed Redeemer has called, and qualified us to long and aspire after, in these words: "Thy kingdom come; Thy will be done, on earth, as it is in heaven." It is to be sought for in the simplicity of a little child, without being captivated with any mysterious depths or heights of speculation; without coveting any knowledge, or wanting to see any ground of nature, grace, or creature, but so far as it brings us nearer to God, forces us to forget and renounce everything for Him; to do everything in Him, with Him, and for Him; and to give every breathing, moving, stirring, intention, and desire of our heart, soul, spirit, and life to Him.

Let every creature have your love. Love with its fruits of meekness, patience, and humility, is all that we can wish for to ourselves, and our fellow-creatures; for this is to live in God, united to Him, both for time and eternity.

To desire to communicate good to every creature, in the degree we can, and it is capable of receiving from us, is a divine temper; for thus God stands unchangeably disposed towards the whole creation: but let me add my request, as you value the peace which God has brought forth by His Holy Spirit in you, as you desire to be continually taught by an unction from above, that you would on no account enter into any dispute with anyone about the truths of salvation; but give them every help, but that of debating with them; for no man has fitness for the light of the gospel, till he finds an hunger and thirst, and want of something better, than that which he has and is by nature. Yet we ought not to check our inclinations to help others in every way we can. Only do what you do, as a work of God; and then, whatever may be the event, you will have reason to be content with the success that God gives it. "He that hath ears to hear, let him hear;" may be enough for you, as well as it was for our blessed Lord.

The next thing that belongs to us, and which is also godlike, is a true unfeigned patience, and meekness, showing every kind of goodwill and tender affection towards those that turn a deaf ear to us; looking upon it to be full as contrary to God's method, and the good state of our own heart, to dispute with anyone in contentious words, as to fight with him for the truths of salvation.

"Come unto Me, all ye that labour and are heavy laden, and I will give you rest," saith our blessed Lord. He called none else, because no one else hath ears to hear, or a heart to receive the truths of redemption.

Hear what our blessed Lord saith, of the place, the power, and origin of truth. He refers us not to the current doctrines of the times, or to the systems of men, but to His own name, His own nature, His own divinity hidden in us: "My sheep," says He, "hear My voice." Here the whole matter is decisively determined, both where truth is, and who they are that can have any knowledge of it.

Heavenly truth is nowhere spoken but by the voice of Christ, nor heard but by the power of Christ living in the hearer. As He is the eternal only Word of God, that speaks forth all the wisdom, and wonders of God; so He alone is the word, that speaks forth all the life, wisdom, and goodness, that is or can be in any creature; it can have none but what it has in Him and from Him. This is the one unchangeable boundary of truth, goodness, and every perfection of men on earth, or angels in heaven.

Literary learning, from the beginning to the end of time, will have no more of heavenly wisdom, nor any less of worldly foolishness in it, at one time than at another; its nature is one and the same through all ages; what it was in the Jew and the heathen, that same it is in the Christian. Its name, as well as nature, is unalterable, namely, foolishness with God.

I shall add no more, but the two or three following words.

I. Receive every inward and outward trouble, every disappointment, pain, uneasiness, temptation, darkness, and desolation, with both thy hands, as a true opportunity and blessed occasion of dying to self, and entering into a fuller fellowship with thy self-denying, suffering Saviour.

II. Look at no inward or outward trouble in any other view; reject every other thought about it; and then every kind of trial and distress will become the blessed day of thy prosperity.

III. Be afraid of seeking or finding comfort in anything, but God alone. For that which gives thee comfort, takes so much of thy heart from God. "Quid est Cor purum? cui ex toto, et pure sufficit solus Deus, cui nihil sapit, quod nihil delectat, nisi Deus." That is, What constitutes a pure heart? One to which God alone is totally, and purely sufficient; to which nothing relishes, or gives delight, but God alone.

IV. That state is best, which exerciseth the highest faith in, and fullest resignation to God.

V. What is it you want and seek, but that God may be all in all in you? But how can this be, unless all creaturely good and evil becomes as nothing in you, or to you?

"Oh Anima mea, abstrahe te ab Omnibus. Quid tibi cum mutabilibus Creaturis? Solum Sponsum tuum, qui omnium est Author Creaturarum, expectans, hoc age, ut Cor tuum ille liberum et expeditum semper inveniat, quoties illi ad ipsum venire placuerit." That is, O my soul! abstract thyself from everything. What hast thou to do with changeable creatures? Waiting and expecting thy bridegroom, who is the author of all creatures, let it be thy sole concern. that He may find thy heart free and disengaged, as often as it shall please Him to visit thee.

Be assured of this, that sooner or later, we must be brought to this conviction, that everything in ourselves by nature is evil, and must be entirely given up; and that nothing that is creaturely, can make us better than we are by nature. Happy, therefore, and blessed are all those inward or outward troubles, that hasten this conviction in us; that with the whole strength of our souls, we may be driven to seek all from and in God, without the least thought, hope, or contrivance after any other relief. Then it is, that we are made truly partakers of the cross of Christ; and from the bottom of our hearts shall be enabled to say, with St. Paul, "God forbid that I should glory in anything, save the cross of our Lord Jesus Christ: by which I am crucified to the world, and the world is crucified to me."

Give up yourself to God without reserve. This implies such a state or habit of heart, as does nothing of itself, from its own reason, will or choice, but stands always in faith, hope, and absolute dependence upon being led by the Spirit of God into everything that is according to His will; seeking nothing by designing,

reasoning, and reflection, how you shall best promote
the honour of God, but in singleness of heart, meeting
everything that every day brings forth, as something
that comes from God, and is to be received, and gone
through by you, in such an heavenly use of it, as you
would suppose the Holy Jesus would have done, in
such occurrences. This is an attainable degree of
perfection; and by having Christ and His Spirit
always in your eye, and nothing else, you will never
be left to yourself, nor without the full guidance of God.

LETTER XXV.

20. How Good and Evil are both from God.

Concerning the following texts, God hardened the
heart of Pharaoh : "He hath mercy on whom He will
have mercy, and whom He will He hardeneth";
"Good and evil are from the Lord"; "I create light,
and I create darkness"; you ask, how these things
can be consistently affirmed of a God, all love and
goodness to His creatures ?

All the difficulty of reconciling such contrary things
as are said of God, that He willeth only life and good,
and yet that evil and death, are said to come from
Him, arises from our considering the operations of
God in a creaturely manner, or as we should understand the same contrary things, if they were affirmed
of any creature. Whereas the operation of God, in
its whole kind and nature, is as different from anything that can be done by creatures, as the work and
manner of creation, is different, in power, nature, and

manner, from that which creatures can do to one another. For (N.B.) the operation of God is never in or with the creature in any other manner, or doing any other thing, but that which it was and did in the creation of them. This, and this alone is the working of the Deity in heaven and on earth; nothing comes from Him, or is done by Him through all the eternity of His creatures, but that essential manifestation of Himself in them, which began the glory and perfection of their first existence. Now from this one, single, immutable operation of God, that He can be nothing else in, or towards the creature, but that same love and goodness, that He was to it, at its creation, it necessarily follows, that to the creature that turns from Him, God can be nothing else to it, but the cause of all its evil and miserable state. Hence is that of the apostle, that "Sin cometh by the law, because where there is no law, there is no transgression." Now God, or the divine nature in man, is the one great law of God in man, from which, all that is good and all that is evil in him, hath its whole state and nature. His life can have no holiness or goodness in it, but as the divine nature within him, is the law by which he lives. He can commit no other sin, nor feel any kind of hurt or evil from it, but what comes from resisting, or rebelling against that of God, which is in him; and therefore the good and evil of man, are equally from God. And yet this could not be, but because of this ground, namely, that God is unchangeable love and goodness, and has only one will and work of love and goodness towards the creature. Just as the law could not make sin, or evil, but because it has no sin or evil in itself, but is im-

mutably righteous, holy, and good, and has only one will
and one work towards man, whether he receives good
or evil by it. Therefore the righteous, holy law, that
is so, because it never changes its goodwill, and work
towards man, can truly say of itself these two contrary things, I create good, and I create evil, without
the least contradiction. In the like truth, and from
the same ground, it must be said, that happiness and
misery, life and death, tenderness and hardness of
heart, are from God, or because God is that which He
is, in and to the birth and life of man.

This is the one true key to the state of man before
his fall, to his state after his fall, and to the whole
nature of his redemption. All which three states, are
in a few words of our Saviour, set forth in the clearest
and strongest degree of light. " I am the true vine,
ye are the branches. He that abideth in Me, and I in
him, bringeth forth much fruit." This was man's first
created state of glory and perfection, it was a living
and abiding in God, such a birth and communion of
life with Him, and from Him, as the branch hath in
and from the vine.

The nature of man's fallen state, and whence he has
all the evil that is in it, is set forth in the following
words, " If a man abide not in Me " (the true vine)
" he is cast forth as a branch, and is withered, and
men gather them, and they are cast into the fire and
burned." This comprehends the whole of man's fallen
state, namely, a being broken off from the life of God,
and therefore become such a poor, withered, helpless
creature, as may have all that done to him, as a fire-
brand of hell and devils, which men may do to a
broken off, withered branch of the vine. And his

state is as different from that of his creation, as a withered branch, smoking and burning in the fire, is different from its first state of life and growth in the rich spirit of the vine.

Again, the whole of man's redeemed state, is in the following words :—" I am the bread of life, that came down from heaven ;—He that eateth this bread shall live for ever ;—whoso eateth My flesh and drinketh My blood, hath eternal life,—dwelleth in Me, and I in him." This is our whole redemption, it consists in nothing else, but having the full life of God, or birth of Christ begotten, and born in us again. And thus do these three states of man fully show, that our first perfection, our miserable fall, and blessed redemption, have all that they have in them, whether of glory, or misery, merely and solely because God alone is all that is good, and can be nothing else but good towards the creature; and that neither angel nor man can be happy or miserable, but because it either hath, or hath not, this one God of goodness essentially living and operating in it.

What a number of things called religion, are here cut off at once ? since nothing is life, happiness, and glory, but the one essential operation of the triune God of love, and goodness within us; nothing is death, evil, or misery, but the departure, or turning from this essential God of our lives, to something that we would have from ourselves, or the creatures that are about us. And how greatly is he deluded, who living among the throng of religious schemes, thinks this, or that, or anything in nature, can be his atonement, his reconciliation, and union with God, but the Spirit, the body, and the blood of Christ forming themselves into a new creature within him. Then,

and then only is he that first man that God created,
in whom alone He can be well pleased.   But till then,
he is that man, whom the Cherub's two-edged flaming
sword will not suffer to enter into Paradise.

21. How the Life of God is revealed in us.

How is it now, that we are to regain that first
birth of Christ?   Why just in the same way, as Adam
had it at first.   What did he then do?   How did he
help forward God's creating power?   Now creating
again, or restoring a first life in God, is just the same
thing, and the same sole work of God, as creating us
at first; and therefore we can have no more share of
power in the one, than in the other.   Nothing lies upon
us as creatures fallen from God, or is required of us
with regard to our growth in God, but not to resist
that, which God is doing towards a new creation of us.

That which God is doing towards the new creation
of us, had its beginning before the foundation of the
world.   " In Christ Jesus," saith St. Paul, " we were
chosen before the foundation of the world;" the same
as saying, that God out of His great mercy, had chosen
to preserve a seed of the Word and Spirit of God in
fallen man, which through the mediation of a God
incarnate, should revive into that fulness of stature in
Christ Jesus, in which Adam was at first created.
And all this work of God towards a new creation, is by
that same essential operation of God in us, which at
first created us in His image and likeness.   And
therefore nothing belongs to man in it, but only to
yield himself up to it, and not resist it.

Now who is it, that may be said to resist it?   It is

everyone who does not deny himself, take up his cross daily, and follow Christ. For everything but this, is that flesh that warreth against the Spirit. The whole life of the natural man, resisteth all that essential operation of God, which would create us again in Christ Jesus. Further, every religious man resisteth it, in and by and through the whole course of his religion, who takes anything to be the truth of piety, the truth of devotion, the truth of religious worship, but faith, and hope, and trust, and dependence upon that alone, which the all-creating Word and all-sanctifying Spirit of God, inwardly, essentially, and vitally worketh in his soul.

Would you know, how you are to understand this essential operation of the triune Holy Deity in our souls, and why nothing else is, or can be that grace or help of God, which bringeth salvation, take this earthly similitude of the matter.

The light and air of this world, are universal powers, that are essential to the life of all the creatures of this world. They are essential, because nothing sees, till the light has brought forth a birth of itself in the essence of the creature, which birth of light can last no longer, than it is essentially united with the operation of that universal light which brought it forth. Air is also essential to the life of the creature, because nothing lives, till a birth of the air is born in it, nor any longer, than its own inborn air, is in essential union with that universal air, and operation of air, that first brought it forth. Now from this essential, unalterable relation between light and air, and seeing, living creatures, it plainly follows, that darkness and death, may be ascribed to them, as well as seeing and life.

Thus, if light and air could say anything of themselves in outward words, of that which they are, and
do to all animals; if the light was to say, It is I that
make seeing and blind eyes; if the air was to say, I
create life, and I create death; could there be any
difficulty of understanding, or allowing the truth of
these words ? Or could they be true in any other
sense, but because where light is not, there is the cause
of darkness, and where air is not, there is the cause of
death. And so in the strictest truth of the words,
seeing and blind eyes are from the light; living and dead
bodies are from the air. Because darkness could not
be, but because light does not shine in it, nor the body be
dead, but because the breathing of the air is not in it.

It is thus, with the essential operation of the triune
Holy God, in the life of all divine and godly creatures,
whether men or angels. The light and Holy Spirit of
God, are universal powers, and essential to the birth
of a godly life in the creature; which creaturely birth
of a divine life, can begin no sooner, than the **Word**
and **Spirit** of God bring forth a birth of themselves in
the creature, nor subsist any longer, than it is united
with, and under the continual operation of that Word
and Spirit, which brought it forth. Hence it is truly
said, that spiritual life, and spiritual death, spiritual
good and spiritual evil, happiness and misery are from
God, and that for this one reason, because there is no
good, but in God, nor any other operation of God in,
and to the creature, but that of heavenly life, light,
love, and goodness.

When man, created in the image and likeness of
God, to be an habitation and manifestation of the
triune God of goodness, had by the perverseness of a

false will, turned from his holy state of life in God, and so was dead to the blessed union, and essential operation of God in his soul, yet the goodness of God towards man, altered not, but stood in the same good-will towards man as at the first, and willed, and could will nothing else towards the whole human nature, but that every individual of it, might be saved from that state of death and misery in an earthly nature, into which they were fallen.

Hence, that is, from this unchangeable love of God towards man, which could no more cease, than God could cease, came forth that wonderful scene of providence, of such a variety of means, and dispensations, of visions, voices, and messages from heaven, of law, of prophecies, of promises and threatenings, all adapted to the different states, conditions, and ages of the fallen world, for no other end, but by every art of divine wisdom, and contrivance of love, to break off man from his earthly delusion, and beget in him a sense of his lost glory, and so make him capable of finding again that blessed essential operation of Father, Son, and Holy Spirit in his soul, which was the essential glory of his first creation.

Now, as in this scene of a divine and redeeming providence, God had to do with a poor, blind, earthly creature, that had lost all sense of heavenly things, as they are in themselves, so the wisdom of God, must often, as it were humanise itself, and condescend to speak of Himself after the manner of men. He must speak of His eyes, His ears, His hands, His nose, etc., because the earthly creature, the mere natural man, could no otherwise be brought into any sense of that, which God was to him.

But now, all this process of divine providence, was only for the sake of something higher; the mystery of God in man, and man in God, still lay hid, and was no more opened, than the mystery of a redeeming Christ, was opened in the type of a Paschal lamb.

Pentecost alone was that, which took away all veils, and showed the kingdom of God, as it was in itself, and set man again under the immediate, essential operation of God, which first gave birth to a holy Adam in Paradise. Types and shadows ended, because the substance of them was found. The cloven tongues of fire had put an end to them, by opening the divine eyes, which Adam had closed up, unstopping the spiritual ears, that he had filled with clay, and making his dumb sons to speak with new tongues.

And what did they say? They said all old things were gone, that a new heaven and a new earth were coming forth, that God Himself was manifested in the flesh of men, who were now all taught of God. And what were they taught? That same which Adam was taught by his first created life in God, namely, that the immediate, essential operation of Father, Son, and Holy Spirit, was henceforth the birthright of all that were become true disciples of Christ. Thus ended the old creation, and the fall of man, in a God manifested in the flesh, dying in and for the world, and coming again in Spirit, to be the life and light of all the sons of Adam.

OTHER QUALITY BOOKS FROM BETHANY FELLOWSHIP

ANDREW MURRAY BOOKS

Be Perfect	$1.45
Day by Day with Andrew Murray	$1.25
Holy in Christ	$2.45
How to Raise Your Children for Christ	$3.50
Jesus Christ: Prophet-Priest	.75
Like Christ	$1.45
New Life	$1.45